PAUL MOMPREMIER

PRINCE MOTIVATION

How a boy became a man without guidance

Paul Mompremier | July 2017

To: Lillian

From: Paul Mompremier

Thank you for your support. You have been such a beautiful person for so many years. I hope you enjoy and read the book from beginning to end. I wish you great health, wealth, and success.

Prince Motivation

Create Space, a DBA of On-Demand Publishing, LLC.

Editor: Maureen O'Hara

Proofreader: Alexis Fils-Aime

Printed in the United States of America

ISBN-13: 978-0-692-88507-9

ISBN-10: 0692885072

To my mother, my father, my sister, my brother,

To all my friends who became family

Acknowledgement

First and Foremost, I must give all praise to the most high Allah "God" for given me the strength to write my truth, my story, and have the courage to share it with you all. To my mother who I try to make proud every second I'm alive. Who raised me as a single mother and gave up so much to watch me grow and become the man she wanted me to be. To my grandfather, R.I.P Paul Mompremier who you will get to learn about later in this book. My sister Alexis for just being loving and always supportive of your big brother. To everyone who encouraged me to complete this book even when I felt like quitting. To everyone who purchased the first wave of shirts before I completed the book, off the strength you knew I was going to be successful. To my father who I grown to have a relationship with over the years before it was too late. To all my friends that are family in my eyes whom are mention in the book. To the nay sayers who fueled me and gave me the energy and a name for this emotion and passion I call Prince Motivation. To my second mom Sabne Noel for pushing me. To the people, I worked with who ever had anything positive to say about me. Broward County the schools, parks, boys and girls club I attended. The Urban League of Broward County who taught me how to be a great leader. Bishop TD Jakes, Oprah, Tyler Perry, Steve Harvey, Honorable Minister Louis Farrakhan, Malcom X, Kevin Gates, Boosie, Tupac Shakur, Kobe Bryant, Eric Thomas, and Charlemagne the God, for inspiring me!

Table of Contents

Introduction

A self-publish autobiography of a driven young author named Paul Mompremier. The self-proclaimed Prince of Broward County Florida shows readers how to tap into their God-given talents to achieve ultimate success. He uses his life as an example, and takes readers on a journey thru adversity, vital relationships, different work environments, and many other obstacles he faced throughout his life, and how he became the man he is today.

Whether it was hip hop music, the streets, beautiful women, or materialistic things; he found motivation in key life events which culminated in what he now calls "Prince Motivation". Along this journey, he experienced his heart break, ended up homeless, and longed for guidance. He made mistakes, made the best out of his situation and found people along the way to show him that he could do anything he set his mind to.

Comparing his own social, business and personal examples to that of celebrities, Mompremier shows readers how to rediscover their natural aptitude and how to extract wisdom from their past experiences. Knowing when to let people go in life, when to take a risk, and when to listen to your heart will become possible once you un cover the motivation that God gave them.

He is a man that represents the working middle class with a typical nine to five. He may not be the smartest person in the room. He may not have had a privilege lifestyle as others, but he can relate to everyone in his community. He will give readers the blueprint to achieve anything they want in life. Paul Mompremier is on his way to becoming the next best motivational speaker and author. With Prayer, Patience, and Persistence in your everyday life he will show that Prince Motivation is key!

CHAPTER 1 A PRINCE WAS BORN

The Year 1984 is a very memorable year. First off you had the year of the jheri curl. The year of pop and fashion. Super Bowl XVIII: the LA Raiders beat Washington Red Skins, 38 to 9 in the Tampa Super Bowl. The game's MVP award went to Marcus Allen, LA Raiders, running back. Hulk Hogan defeated Iron Sheik to become WWF champ! Michael Jackson was burned during filming for a Pepsi commercial. President Ronald Reagan formally announced he would seek a second term and won by a landslide, winning 49 states. Carl Lewis jumped a world record indoor, and won the gold medal in 100-meter dash at LA Summer Olympics. Carl also won his second (long jump) of four gold medals in the Summer Olympics. Carl Lewis won three (200m) of four gold medals. Michael Jackson won eight Grammys! NFL Baltimore Colts moved to Indianapolis. Kareem Abdul-Jabbar broke Wilt Chamberlain's all-time career scoring record of 31,419 points! South African prisoner Nelson Mandela saw his wife for the first time in 22 years! Prince Charles called a proposed addition to the National Gallery, London, a "monstrous carbuncle on the face of a much-loved and elegant friend," sparking controversy on the role of the Royal Family and course of modern architecture. Boston Celtics beat the LA Lakers four games to three. Vanessa Williams, the first African-American Miss America, resigned due to posing nude. Walter Payton broke the NFL's career rushing record, passing one of my favorite running backs of all time, Jim Brown on October 7, 1984. Beverly Hills Cop, directed by Martin Brest and starring Eddie Murphy and Judge Reinhold, premiered in Los Angeles. Prince was a superstar who I respected. He was the epitome of a living legend. I dreamed of being a living legend, so at a very young age, I tattooed "Living Legend" on my biceps as a reminder of who I should be. Prince is my nickname, but the musician Prince was an American singer-songwriter, multi-instrumentalist, and record producer. He was a musical innovator who was known for his eclectic work, flamboyant stage presence, extravagant dress and makeup, and wide vocal range. His music integrated a wide variety of styles, including funk, rock, R&B, new wave, soul, psychedelia, and pop. He has sold over 100 million records worldwide, making him one of the best-selling artists of all time. He won seven Grammy Awards, an American Music Award, a Golden Globe Award, and an Academy Award for the film Purple Rain. He was inducted into the Rock and Roll Hall of Fame in 2004, his first year of eligibility. Rolling Stone ranked Prince at number 27 on its list of 100 Greatest Artists, "the most influential artists of the rock & roll era." With all these amazing facts that happened in 1984, the most important fact and date you should know is that a legend, a leader, a hustler, a motivator, handsome, charming, and good-looking baby was born that year.

On July 5th, 1984, Rosana Mompremier gave birth to her son, Me!! (Kolyon voice), Paul Mompremier, Jr. at Jackson Memorial Hospital in Dallas, Texas. She named me after her father, Paul Mompremier. I was her second child, but the first to survive. My mother was pregnant once before but lost the baby. She used to tell me all the time "You were supposed to have an older brother, but he passed away". My mom was born in Port-au-Prince, Haiti. She lived there, being raised by her mom, my grandmother. My grandmother was a hard-working, strict parent raising my mom and her brother. My mother use to tell me all the time that she had it rough growing up. My mom couldn't have a boyfriend because she would just go to school, come home, and do her chores. Every time my mother would back talk to my grandmother, she would get a good third-world country beating for disobeying her mom. If anyone in the community knew my grandmother and saw my mother or uncle do anything bad, they would beat them. My mother told me my grandmother was strict on her because she didn't want my mother to get pregnant at an early age. One day my mom would get to go to live with my grandfather in the United States of America, and he would send her a visa. My grandmother just wanted my mom to go the USA a virgin. Well, my mother end up getting pregnant by her boyfriend at the time and had the baby. She ended up leaving her baby behind to be raised by my grandmother and her boyfriend's family. That was one of the toughest decisions my mother had to make 2 weeks after having the baby. Six months later, while my mother was living in New York with my grandfather, the baby was pronounced dead because of medical reasons. So, I never got to meet my older sibling. Sometimes I can see in my mother's eyes, and I see why she loves me so much. I can tell when she looks at me that she is proud to have a surviving strong son in me.

I never knew what having a big brother would feel like until I became one. Three years later, my mother gave birth to my precious sister, Alexis Fils-Aime. I was now a big brother and was responsible for looking after a young girl and protecting her from anything bad in life. Me and my sister Alexis have had the best of times with each other. We were typical kids, always with each other. We attended the same schools. We always played with each other whether it was tearing up the house, playing Super Market sweep with whatever was in the fridge. We acted like we were wrestlers. I was Razor Ramon, and she was Macho Man Randy savage! R.I.P by the way. If I ever made her cry, she would call my mom while at work, and my mom would say she was going to give me a whopping when she got home. Alexis was a little tattled tell, but I loved her; she was my best friend. Growing up, I made sure she could not be around boys I didn't know as well. Alexis and I would talk about anything, and I was a little jealous of her. She was always getting good grades, coming home always did her homework, and getting straight A's and B's! I was ok with some subjects, but Alexis was that little sister who would get picked up from school and be all jolly when report cards came out. I would get in the car and try to keep the report cards a secret, and here she goes all smiles, "We got report cards today"! She was so disrespectful and a bragger that she would have gotten all A's and B's, and I would get the rest B's, C's, maybe a D, but never an F, though! I never took school seriously. I just went and did what I had to do to pass. The only subject that caught my attention was math.

I remember vividly growing up in Dallas. We didn't have much family there. Other than my mother and sister, I only had an uncle and my grandfather. My uncle, Paulemond, was very serious. He was always a family man, always calm. I didn't see him that much, and I don't think he was a fan of Alex, who was my step dad. Like any big brother, he always thought he had to protect my mother. He always felt my mom deserved a much better man than Alex. She married Alex in Dallas, Texas, at the courthouse. She didn't really get her dream wedding that some women dream of having! Alex was a skinny, Canadian man who was kind of a loner. To me, he was soft spoken but played hard in the house. I would watch football, basketball, or even wrestling on TV, and he would just come and switch the channel to hockey! I would look at him pissed and go to my room and maybe play video games. I felt as a kid that he never showed me love. Back then, he was like a step dad, but I looked at him like he was a dad. I didn't understand why he loved Alexis more than me. We never played sports together or watched them together. He never took me to games or even my own extra-curricular activities with sports. It would always be my friend's parents or coaches. We never ever clicked, and I don't really know why? I never called him dad; it was always Alex.

We lived with my grandfather's wife Lutane Mompremier when I was a baby. She loved my grandfather to death and would do anything for him. Lutane was very protective of my grandfather and showed him a lot of love. I know now, but back then, Lutane could not have kids, so I guess that made her the way she was. She wasn't happy to have my mother, my sister, and me living under her roof because of the profound love she had for my grandfather, she accepted us. She made it known to my mother that she didn't like us by her comments and behavior. My mother had it rough there, but she remained strong. She continued to work every day, take care of two kids, and dealt with my sister's father infidelities. Alex was caught sleeping with my mom's best friend, who was also Alexis's godmother. Crazy, right! She stayed with him because he told her repeatedly that he wouldn't hurt her again. He always promised her that he would get her a house in Garland, and she believed and forgave him. It was 1991 when we moved to Garland, around the same time that Rodney King got beaten up by the police.

The house was very nice and spacious, and It holds a lot of great memories there for me. We used to have Super Bowl parties there, which is where I became a football fan of the hometown Dallas Cowboys. Watching the "Playmaker" Michael Irvin, the best running back I have ever seen, Emmitt Smith, the best cornerback, "Primetime" Deion Sanders and company win back-to-back Super Bowls! I'm still mad they didn't draft Randy Moss, but let me continue with my life story. My grandfather used to come to the new house sometimes and always played with me and Alexis and always made us smile. He would play football with me in the big back yard we had. He would chase me around and just spend time with me. He was clearly a great father figure. Something else that I remember about my grandfather, he was sure a lady's man; he adored beautiful women. He had a girlfriend that lived five houses from our house down the street on Maydelle Lane in Garland, Texas. One day, when I was about 7 years old, I saw my grandfather and his girlfriend driving in a car and pass my house, laughing and waving at me; they looked so happy. It was the last time I would see my grandfather alive. That night my mother received a call to come to the hospital because my grandfather had a heart attack. I remember my whole family running to the hospital to find him on a stretcher with blood all over his body. It was reported that he had suffered a cardiac arrest. My family was furious to find out that my grandfather waited in the lobby in excruciating pain before the staff attended to him. They announced that he was dead later that night. My family ended up suing the hospital for negligence and won. I was later and still to this day scared of hospitals.

My mother and uncle inherited a great amount of money. My Uncle packed up and moved to South Florida. My mom bought a brand-new Honda with no miles on it; it smelled so good. She also took a trip back to her country: Haiti. That trip was very humbling for me; she wanted Alexis and me to meet my grandmother. It was an opportunity to live and visit a third world country and see how people lived daily without the bare necessities. A country with no government, no light, and where one must take long walks to go get water from rivers just so that we can drink and bathe with. I saw houses the size of my bedroom and people with missing body parts begging for money everywhere, even at the airport. Everyone in my mom's family treated her like a queen, I'm guessing because they hadn't seen her for so long. They also had their hands out, for they were sure that my mother was rich. My mom went down there and was vulnerable to everyone that gave her a sob story. My maternal grandmother, loved me to death; she treated me like a prince. She made sure my bath water was nice, clean, and warm.

Something we take for granted now became a big deal, something grand. I felt like a real prince like "Really, Really" (Kevin Gates). When I was hungry, she gave me peanut butter sandwiches. Whenever I was thirsty, I got a bottle of soda like Coke, Sprite, or whatever I asked for. She was so proud of my mom and happy to see her. I believe she had not seen my mom since she left to move to America. I was already 7, so it had to be like 8 years since she last laid eyes on her daughter.

If I can remember, my mom has always been a giving person. She gave to the poor and her family, yet the more she gave, the more they wanted from her. I was young, but I was no fool. I learn to see BS from a mile away at a very young age. The heat, mosquito bumps, and showering in public made me decide that living in Haiti is real tough. Seeing people's ribs and empty stomach daily made my stomach hurt. We used to ride on the back of people's trucks; they call them taxis. Grown people use to just give me they middle finger and say, "American" with a mean look on their faces! I told my mother I'll never go back there; they don't like me. I had no choice, so she took me there another time; it wasn't that bad the second time around. I had fun, and they treated me like a prince. Visiting Haiti made me appreciate the little things I take for granted. I believe every person nationwide should go to a third world country and be humbled of how blessed we are and how many things we take for granted. I still to this day barely complain about anything because I know somebody somewhere has it 10 times worse than me.

Back in Garland, I attended Beaver Elementary where I excelled in math, which was my favorite subject. I could do math problems in my head within seconds and won competitions. One day, I was in class, and my math teacher told the class she wanted to play a game. We would have 5 minutes to answer as many questions as we could without working them out in our heads. I was very competitive and a well-known trash talker in my class, so I wanted to win. I ended up winning and represented my class and school at a public-school competition! I end up winning third in the city, but was mad I didn't get first place. I end up growing a passion to love math. My sister and I always won the award for perfect attendance as well. It was a guarantee we were going to school whether we were sick or tired; not going to school wasn't an option. I believe all parents from any foreign country or island really have a passion for education. We loved going to school, except for times when my Mom come thru jamming Kompa music loud in her car. You could hear the music playing blocks away with loud drums, and we would walk with our heads down in embarrassment. My mother made me love and appreciate music at a young age. I think that's where I get jamming in the car blasting music from. She used to play a lot of Bob Marley, and she introduce me to Rap. One day we went to Best Buy and she bought me a boom box.

With a Tupac, Kriss Kross, Immature, Biggie, and Bone Thugs and Harmony CD! That's when I fell in love with Hip-Hop! I bet many people can't say they sat in a car with their mother and spit Tupac lyrics in the car every other day. My mother loved artists like T Vice and Sweet Mickey as well.

Around this time, I used to spend my weekends at Johnny's house, who was a man that I later found out was my father. He lived in Oak Cliff, Texas, 45 minutes from Garland in Dallas, Texas. It was a rough neighborhood. All I did when I was with Johnny was go to the parks with him, watched a lot of street car races with fast cars, and went fishing. I wasn't good at fishing, but I loved seeing fast cars. That is probably why I love the Monte Carlo SS by Chevy. Throughout the week, I would live with my mom, Alexis, and my sister's dad Alex. Alex always treated my younger sister Alexis nice and wishy-washy with me. Sometimes, I was Alex's best friend, then sometimes, I felt like he hated me. He would give me money to go buy a Big Mac Meal from McDonalds (yea, I loved that growing up). He was very unpredictable; randomly, he would just be evil. It's like he was bipolar. One day, I was riding my bike with training wheels in the garage, and I rode in a circle, lap after lap. He was in the garage as well; my riding my bike riding in a circle lap after lap may have irritated him. He slammed down the garage door, causing glass to shatter all over my leg. I screamed and yelled, and he just stood there; he showed no compassion. I had big chunk of my skin gone, and all one could see was white meat and blood everywhere. My mom came in yelling and crying, and they rushed me to the nearest hospital. I was in excruciating pain because my leg was split open, covered in a bath towel soaked in blood. They argued in the car because Alex wanted to drive miles away to a hospital that he and my mom worked at instead of one nearby. They gave me a shot in my leg inside the white meat and stitched my leg up. I took my shot in the leg like a G. I sustained a laceration that took 20 stitches to close, and I still have the mark today. It was that moment when I realized Alex didn't care about me. Its certain things that happen in your childhood that you will never forget.

CHAPTER 2 STEP DAD FROM HELL

One day at Beaver Elementary, I pulled my pants down in the cafeteria and told a girl to look at my privates under the lunch table! A girl ran and told one of my teachers. The teacher told me to go to the principal's office, and all the kids in the cafeteria at the same time were like "Ewe

. . . "I went to the principal's office, and he question me about what happen? I admitted to pulling my pants down because I didn't think it was a bad thing. I must remind you that I have become a big fan of music and used to see Bobby Brown dance and pull his pants down. My principal told me to assume position as he pulled out one of those old-school paddles. I'm looking at him crazy like you are not about to whoop me. I was mouthing off saying you aint my daddy! They had to call the PE teacher in the principal's office to hold me down. I was running all around the office, and long story short, they said they were going to tell my parents when they picked me up. My teacher told me that I couldn't perform in the talent show that year. I was going to perform a Michael Jackson song, and now I couldn't for being bad. I was a big fan of Michael Jackson growing up. I had a pair of penny loafers, and I used to do the moonwalk all around the house in those shoes. I believe I can still do the moonwalk to this day. One time, I was in the kitchen while my mom was mopping the floor and bust my head open trying to spin in a circle impersonating the King of Pop. I got the scar on my head to prove it. I'm still to this day a little dancer. I love dancing and having fun.

So, they put a pin with a note on my shirt to see the teacher when Alex came to picked me up. I ripped it off and threw it away. The teacher saw me rip off the note and walked with me to the car and told Alex what I did. Well, as soon as I got home, Alex told me to go in my room. I went in the room, and like any other kid would do, I hid. Alex came in that room and closed the door real slow. I tried to out run him, but there was nowhere to go. He beat me to death like I was a slave caught sleeping with the master's daughter with a black leather belt. I cried and kept saying, "Ok, I'm sorry; I won't do it again, but he would not stop. He beat me so badly that the leather belt broke and ripped in half. He beat me until I was blue, black, and purple! I cried and sat in tears of anger because I knew if my grandfather were still living, he would've never put his hands on me. I just couldn't wait to tell my mom what Alex did! I played tough when he was done and stayed quiet. I had a plan; if I played it cool and didn't say anything, he would think I wouldn't say nothing. The plan was to stay cool until he picked my mom up, and soon as he picked her up and she got in the car, I was going to cry and tell her what Alex did.

He came in the room and said, "Let's go pick up your mom. As we walked to the car, he had the belt in his hand. I'm like, dang, this dude still aint done whopping me? He threw the belt in the trunk and tried to hide the evidence. We drove to the hospital, and it was a long ride. I would see him look in his rear-view mirror at me, giving me dirty looks. He picked my mom up from work, and she got in the car, and I let it rip. I cried as loud as I could. My skin was black and purple with bruises, and she said, "What happen to you?" I said Alex beat me with the belt in trunk. She looked at him and said, "Why did you hit my son"? He told her what the teacher said, and she said, "I don't care; you don't hit my son." Then, he stopped the car and slapped her in the car and said, "What you going to do about it?" I froze and paused and couldn't believe for the first time that I've seen this man hit my mother. I remember hearing her say that she is going to show the police when we get home. We arrived home, and she did nothing. I was in a state of shock; I've never seen a man hit a woman. This is where I witnessed domestic violence for the first time. It was all my fault; my plan back fired on me, and I ended hurting my mom. As a kid, right then and there, I vowed to never put my hands on a woman. It is the worst thing you can do to a girl or a woman. People laugh and joke about Ike and Tina Turner and Ray Rice and his wife. All jokes aside, the women who stay with that man, who physically hurts you and messes you up emotionally, I pray for you. It scares you for life and can have a trickling effect on your household. My advice is run like Usain right up out of that relationship.

The love that a woman has for her child is amazing. Whether it is single mom or a mom that lets another male figure in the child's life, it should be respected and appreciated that no love is stronger. I see now that I am all grown up why people came up with the phrase "momma's boy." I will always love my mother for always standing up for me. I made a promise to myself to never hit a woman. No man has the right to put his hands on a woman unless it's to comfort or make love to her. I will never forget all the pain Alex has cemented in my mother's life. My mom has a great memory; she doesn't really let go of the bad that has happen to her. It wears on her and has stop her from progressing in life.

After that, Alex thought he was a tough guy. He began to beat on my mom every time she said anything he didn't like. I witness him put Vicks under my mother eyes and have her look straight into a hallway light in our house. I watch this tall, skinny man beat my mother, and I couldn't do anything. Do you know how that felt watching my mother get beat up, and I couldn't stop it? My mother was very strong; she would go the next day to work with makeup on and act like nothing happen. My mom worked at Presbyterian Hospital in Dallas in the laundry unit. She was very popular and always worked hard with a smile on her face; her work ethic to me was amazing. I sometimes feel that is where I get my work ethic from. She worked hard for every dollar she earned. She never did anything illegal to make money; she always worked with integrity. I believe when you come from a third world country, you appreciate having a job a lot more. Every time my mom got her check, she would give me an allowance and buy me nice clothes and shoes. She will and always spent her money on me and got me nice silk shirts from JCPenny. I used to get compliments from my all my teachers. One day, I was playing at recess and one of my teachers asked me jokingly "Paul, can I borrow your nice shirt?" I replied, "No, you can wear your bra...!" I got sent to the principal's office again, but they let me slide.

I remember in 1995, my mom kept telling me something about income tax. She said, whenever she gets it, she will get me anything I want! Around that time, Jason Kidd was the star player for the Dallas Mavericks, and Nike released these nice basketball shoes that looked beautiful. I used to tell all the kids when my momma gets money, she is going to get me those sneakers! I always liked nice sneakers. I had friends who went to Jackson Middle School who had money and always had nice sneakers. So of course, I wanted to fit in and look cool. They were the Nike Air Zoom Flight Black and White that Jason Kidd wore. I wanted them so badly, and the day my mom said, "Ok, let's go get those sneakers you wanted." I jumped up for joy! The mall closest to her job I think now is call Valley View Center. We went right to Foot Locker to get my shoes, laces, shorts, socks, and some shoe cleaner! It was a lot, and I didn't know if my mom was rich, or we just met a good shoe salesman. They used to call Jason Kidd, Jamal Mashburn, and Jimmy Johnson, the Triple J's. They were good, but I was more of a Michael Jordan fan growing up! Michael Jeffrey Jordan, also known by his initials, MJ, is a retired American professional basketball player. He is also a businessman and principal owner and chairman of the Charlotte Hornets. Jordan played 15 seasons in the National Basketball Association for the Chicago Bulls and Washington Wizards. His biography on the NBA website states, "By acclamation, Michael Jordan is the greatest basketball player of all time." Jordan was one of the most effectively marketed athletes of his generation and was considered instrumental in popularizing the NBA around the world in the 1980s and 1990s. The power Michael Jordan has over the sneaker head community sometimes surprises me, but who am I to judge? I love his sneakers, too!

When my mother received her income tax that year, I remember her telling me about bills. She explained to me at a young age that when you grow up, you will make money, but you must take care of your bills. She expressed the importance of making sure the bills were paid and not to have too many. When I would want something and she would tell me no, I knew that it was because of bills. One day, my mother had cash in envelopes all sorted out to pay off all her credit card bills. She was happy, but guess who came and rained on her parade . . . Alex. I watch Alex snatch all the envelopes and take my mother's purse and her money and didn't give it back. It made me hate Alex; yes, hate is a strong word, but I always said in the back of my mind, he will get his day. My mother stayed with him and decided to move down to south Florida when I was 12. I didn't like that idea. I grew up in that neighborhood, I had all my friends, and I just start liking girls. I got my first kiss in Garland, well the first of many. I was the cool black kid that won talent shows at Jackson Middle with my Kris Kross performance. I just began to become popular, and I played baseball there. I had a Spanish baseball coach, and he couldn't pronounce my last name, so he used to call me Primo. I was good in baseball until I got hit with the curve ball that never curved. That baseball smacked me right on my bottom lip; it hurt so badly, I rushed the mound. I would never be the same after that. I was scared to take the mound. I was so scared of pitchers, it made me want to play football. Football was fun. I played D-Line, and fullback my first year, but I just wasn't as good as the skilled players. Eventually I moved to strong safety and running back. So, as you can see, I didn't take moving so well. So, I came up with a plan. When the real estate agent would come to the house to show people our home, I used to play Bone Thugs and Harmony and Tupac songs real loud to point of entering my room loud with gunshots.

So, when they tried to sell the house, they would get scared, and no one would buy the house. That didn't work. Garland was a nice neighborhood. So, they sold the house dirt cheap because Alex was so passionate about opportunities in South Florida. He sold my mom on moving like a used car salesman sells cars. He talked about the beaches and traveling to and from Haiti. My mom believed and trusted him, so we moved. My uncle and Alex drove the truck to Florida, and my sister, my mom, and I flew to Florida. Before we got ready to head to the airport, my mom had a couple of family friends stop by and say bye to us. One guy was named Garcia Desinor, and my family called him Chun. I remember him coming by before we got on the airport shuttle to go catch our flight. He was a funny, cool guy. He had a jheri curl and thought he was God's gift to woman. I remember him picking me up with his son, Junior Desinor, and we went to Toys R' Us and him buying me and his son a wrestling action figure! I didn't see him that much, but he was one of the last people my mom, Alexis, and I remember saying good bye to! It is very important that you remember this story as I continue to tell you about my life.

CHAPTER 3 WELCOME TO BROWARD

So, we arrive to "Deep Side" Lauderhill, FL into the Stonebridge Gardens Condominiums. I looked around the neighborhood, and it look a little rough. It wasn't that bad, but I knew it was not as nice as Garland; it was comparable to Oak Cliff: a little hood, a lot kids and people always outside walking around, or just watching everybody in the community. My uncle and Alex arrived with the big truck, and we unpacked all our belongings. I remember having a GT Dyno bike and leaving it out on our enclosed screen porched. The very next day someone stole it! I was pissed off and knew I didn't like this area. My mom told me we had family here, and they lived very close. They lived like 5 minutes away over a bridge that separated the city of Lauderhill. One side is called Deepside, and the other is Shallow Side! We went to visit my aunt Kettie and her kids, Darnell and Angelica Jean Louis. See, when you grow up, your parents may have a best friend that technically isn't blood, but they call each other brothers and sisters. That automatically made their kids, Darnell and Angelica, now my cousins! They were nice and very cool. Darnell showed me around and introduced me to a neighborhood friend named Delroy. All three of us eventually grew a very tight bond. We all like to play sports, trade athlete playing cards, debate on teams, and tell jokes, which would eventually have us crack on each other (joke or make fun). We were inseparable.

I attended Lauderhill Middle School my seventh-grade year, and I was the new kid on the block. When I first arrived at school on the first day, I thought I was at the school Morgan Freeman took over in the movie "Lean on Me." I saw cliques of all kinds and a lot fights every other day like it was a war zone. I witness a lot of kids my age with marijuana in their book bags pushing at the corner store. I started to see that I was attracted to the mostly ghetto girls. I like the big jewelry they wore and the scent of spritz hair spray and the way they would dance on me at the school dances. When I was in school in Texas, me and my sister Alexis were the only black kids there. Now I was at a school where the population was predominately African-Americans. Boy, did I feel like I was in heaven. I had options when it came to girls (smiling). I never had these emotions and feelings at my school in Texas. So, I felt like I was in heaven. I remember there was one teacher I had on the first day, and his name was Mr. Johnson, a very nice guy. He told me to stand up and introduce myself. I never shied away from anything, so I stood up and said I was from Texas and told the class I was a cool kid. One student told me to ask Mr. Johnson why to do they call him cheesy? I did it and was set up for the kill. Mr. Johnson looked at me now like I was a problem. Apparently, I guess my not knowing the students made fun of him because his pants were always stuck in his butt from being too tight. As soon as I asked that question, all the students bust out laughing. So, Mr. Johnson thought I was trouble, and my classmates thought I was a comedian! So, it kind of worked in my favor.

I met a couple of friends right after that. The word started spreading there is a new country kid from Dallas, Texas. I quickly had a girlfriend that lived in West Wood, and some of my friends lived around her. They were known for beating people up and jumping kids for no reason. I didn't care for fighting people for no reason, so I didn't partake in that. I didn't play sports there although it was like when I came to this school, everybody was in better shape and more athletic than me. I was intimated and didn't even attempt to go try out or sign up for sports. I stuck to pick-up games after school or around the neighborhood because I had a passion for sports and playing in a team setting. One highlight in middle school I remember was my Social Studies teacher gave us an assignment. We had to study how the pilgrims and the Indians came to America! We changed the classroom into a court setting, and my friend Jamie Bryan and I had to represent the pilgrims and the Indians. We were friends, but he was the prosecutor, and I was Johnny Cochran! I respect and love Jamie until this day, but I was trying to win. The teacher was the mediator, and we presented our case. The class was all involved and everyone was engaged. Some students where the jury, and some students were witness or court officials. I hit Jamie with the classic line, "You can't handle the truth," and the class went crazy! I won, and I knew then I had a way with words! I then knew that I found a love for debating truths and facts and standing up for what's right! I still to this day keep in touch with Jamie Bryan and his middle school crush, now wife Nyoka Bryan, thru Facebook. They have a beautiful family!

My seventh-grade year went very smoothly. I had great teachers and met good friends. So, going into the summer of entering 8th grade would be smooth. Boy, was I wrong! During the summer of my seventh-grade year going into my eight-grade year, my mother received news that would change our lives forever. My grandmother past away! I never had seen my mother cry and be so down ever in my life. She cried every day and always asked, Why? My mother did not start working, yet she was living off the money they received from selling our home in Texas. So, with the money she had left, she flew to Haiti to go pay for a funeral and leave money for her family to have while she returned to Florida. So, around that time, I was always at Darnell's house chilling. So, one afternoon, my aunt went to go pick up my mom from the airport. I hadn't seen my mom for like 2 weeks, so I greeted her with a warm hug! She was still down and look very tired. I remember her calling Alex to come pick us up from Kettie's house that evening and her eyes getting big in a state of shock.

Alex told my mother that he would pick up Alexis, but not me and my mom. She looked so confused and again asked, Why? Alex packed up all my mother and my things and packed them in her Honda. He bought another condo just for himself and Alexis while she was gone! So now, my mother and I had nowhere to go; we were now homeless. That man waited and timed his exit perfectly. My mother had no mom, no dad, and no real family because the rest were in Haiti. Kettie took us in and gave us a place to stay while my mom now had to go get a job and provide for me and Alexis. I'm forever grateful to their whole family for taking us in at short notice. I think Alex had a plan to take the money and leave my mom in Florida while he was in the medical field. He quickly started dating another woman in the medical field and had a child with her. My mom was down, and now had to start all over. My mother always had this funny saying. She said life may be rough, but I'm like a cat, and I will always land on my feet. It's kind of funny but true, my mother always found a way to overcome obstacles.

So, my mom met a man named T Will who lived a little down the street from Aunt Kettie's house and let my mom rent two rooms from him while she got back on her feet. It was a good situation for the moment, but money was very tight for my mom. Around this time, school was about to start, and I was entering my eighth-grade year. T Will gave my mother $200 to pay for school clothes and school supplies for me and Alexis. This moment was the one that would change my life. My mother, Alexis, and myself went to Lauderhill Mall. At the time, there was a big Kmart in that mall and a separate entrance to the mall. We got two outfits each from Kmart and walked through the entrance to the mall. On the left, there was a Foot Locker, and on the right, there was a Payless. My mom said, "Let's go." I put my head down and was embarrassed that I was getting sneakers from Payless. I understand the frustration my mom was going through, so I didn't mouth off because I love and respect my mother. Alexis was straight; she got sandals because she was a girl, and I got a pair of fake-looking Jordan's with Shaq dunking on the back of them! I knew then at that age I had to figure out a way to make money. I didn't want my mother to have to worry about money or taking care of me. She already lost enough that year. So, my brain had to think. I was too young to get a real job back then; what was I going to do?

First day of school back then was a holiday for all the kids in my era, maybe nationwide, too. I was so excited to see all my friends and favorite teachers that I didn't get any sleep the night before. The school clothes were ironed and ready to go, all laid out because I felt so fresh and knew I was going to look good. I got a fresh a haircut, and I got to wear my brand-new sneakers! So, we had a ritual. Darnell walked to my house and picked me up, then we both walked to Delroy's house, and from there, we all walked to school. Darnell gave me kind words as he knew our family situation and told me, "Don't worry P, everything will be ok." I had a nice outfit, but I had on some fake Jordan's and just felt down. Delroy noticed, but he was my friend, so he didn't pick on me either. Real friends always will be real friends, no matter the situation. I respect and love them until this day. But boy, when I got to school, I got picked on and laughed about it. Everybody had a joke. I remember one kid named Ronald Mosley say, "Hey Paul, when those Jordan's came out, I aint never see them? You got them at Foot Locker? I went from the cool, new kid to the laughing stock of the school. I was young, and I didn't like it at that age. I was into material things and always wanted to look good. I knew then, I had to figure out a way to make money and make sure that I was accept by my peers.

That week my mother said some shoes came in the mail for me from my dad in Texas. It was a pair of Nikes but they were plain. I never wore those Payless Jordan's again. Right before I left Texas, I had a friend name Demarcus that sold candy for Drug Free America. I went with him a couple of times, and the man gave Demarcus and myself a percentage of what we sold and dropped us home. So, a lightbulb went off in my head! I wonder if there is a Drug Free America here in Florida? I did research asking teachers, friends, and there were no programs called Drug Free America in Fort Lauderdale. To me if there were any city that needed that program it would've been Fort Lauderdale! I didn't want to sell drugs because even though those dudes were getting money, I saw a lot of them get jumped and robbed. There was one kid who was killed, and his body was found in a dumpster by the school, and they had counselors for the whole student body. I didn't want to die or get jumped by the local drug dealers because they played no games. All those D Boys in my city had physique, dreads, gold teeth, and nice cars. I liked the jewelry and like how all the fine girls were attracted to them, so I wanted to make money fast!

So, I start asking some of my friends have they ever heard something like that. Low and behold, I bumped into a kid in class that sold candy, but not for Drug Free America, but for this guy name Brass (R.I.P). Brass would pick kids up after school or on the weekends take them to local malls and high retail areas all over south Florida. Brass would go to a Smart and Final or Sam's Club buy boxes of candy and have the kids sell it. We would wear optimist jerseys for the parks where we played basketball and have a license for selling and sold candy to the public. He would drop us off in high retail areas like big malls or big shopping plazas across South Florida. We would sell M&Ms King Size for $3. Brass would get $2, and we would get $1. We could keep donations so that was a plus. For a while, it was good money. I wasn't shy to speak to people, and I didn't mind working all day, walking around with my friends making money. There would be some nights I came home with $50 to take home, which was good at my age. I started to have money in my pockets. I knew I could have money to get food from the corner store and buy lunch; the school lunch was always nasty. I was now in position to tell my mom I was financially set for food in my body and to pay for school field trips.

Then my hustler's ambition kicked in. I now noticed that Brass would pay $17 for a box, and I was giving him $48 for it because he had the license to sell that was bogus, and he gave me a ride to the mall. He would make fun of all the boys that worked with him sometimes. People know behind every good joke there is some truth to it! He would always say. "Give me my money" and would have "bankrolls" like LiL Boosie would say. I would now become so good at selling and talking to people that I tended to start selling out early! I would call Brass whenever I was finished and tell him to come pick me up, but he wouldn't return my calls. I would start to get scared because I would have nothing to do, and he would pick us up real late. Then on the flip side, I said to myself, well, I got the box already, I got the license, and the jersey, what if I go buy more candy and keep selling while I wait? $$$$ So, some nights Brass would pick me up, and I would say, "Dang, Brass, I only sold 10 M&Ms; here is your $20! So, I would go to Walmart buy more candy and go right outside the building in front and sell them back to the public for $3. Now, I would get the candy for a dollar, and everything I made from that was all mine.

So, now when Brass came pick me up, I gave him $48, and I came home with $100 to $200 a day. I had a drive for selling and hustling. I would never call Brass. I waited for him to call me and find me because he knew my mom was crazy, and he had to bring me home. I know could start buying all my Jordan's from Just for Feet because they will still be on the shelves during the day. I could now buy all the fresh clothes I wanted and still have money for the week to eat at school. I got so good with it, I didn't need Brass any more. He started getting on my nerves, accusing of me of selling my own candy! So, I borrowed one of his licenses and brought my friends Darnell and Delroy onboard. See, my aunt Kettie use to see me and wondered how I was getting all this money? Why you got a pager? She at one point ask my mother was I selling drugs? My mom said no, he is selling candy LOL. She insisted I bring Darnell with me, so he could make money, too. That was my little cousin, and I wanted to see him shine, too. As a matter of fact, I put Delroy in, too, so we all could be fresh! I now created my own little hustle and business. I would go to Smart and Final to buy my box of candy, and I went to Office Depot and print up more licenses and laminate them. Early in the morning with Darnell and Delroy, we would catch the city bus to Sawgrass Mills Mall, and we would sell candy on our own. I never charged them a fee; I just wanted to be around my friends all day and make money together. I was in a good place; I was making money and was now able to maintain keeping myself up and able to buy anything I wanted. I found a way to not sell drugs and make money but work long hours every weekend! My mother now didn't have to buy me anything or even worry about me financially. So, I pretty much funded everything moving forward.

CHAPTER 4 B.A HOME OF THE COBRAS

Well, it's time to start high school, and life at this point is better. My mom had a job working at a hospital in the kitchen because she loved cooking. I was back to being the fresh, cool kid, but I would start high school with my classmates. Delroy was now in the eighth grade and Darnell was in the seventh grade, so they still were at Lauderhill Middle. It was cool though because I was pretty much cool with everybody. Now, I was making money doing my thing on the weekends. My first day at Boyd H. Anderson was cool; I was fresh from head to toe. Wearing Fubu "For Us by Us." I saw a lot of beautiful girls; I was in heaven. Well-shaped and they were everywhere. I now had an attraction to light skin girls; we call them red bones. I got along with everybody my freshman year but went through those typical freshman year experiences. I, too, was victim of being bullied because I wasn't as strong as the upper classmen, being called fresh meat and looking like the babies on campus. All the seniors and upper classmen were bigger than me and got all the girls. I was motivated to try out for sports again. I had a class with legendary coach, David Bowden, and he inspired me to run track. He was pretty much famous for calling kids "Clowns" because he didn't respect kids who didn't take sports seriously. He would say, "MompreAir . . . You're a clown, son; you always making jokes with a smile." He was the best in the building. I believe he told me, "You must get in shape, son, so come out for cross county practice." I'm thinking, what the heck, how hard could running be? After the first practice, I never went back. I quit before I ever got started; I didn't have the courage to face my fears because other kids where bigger and faster and stronger than me. I was scared to play football because all the athletes were bigger and faster.

I was very fortunate to go to school with Michael Frater and see him run! He was from Jamaica and was quiet, nice, funny, and very fast. One-day Coach David D. Bowden took the class out to the track to race one another because he taught personal fitness. Coach David Bowden, ex-NFL player, award winning track athlete, motivational speaker, and coach has dedicated his life to youth! Michael Frater is the fastest human I have ever seen to this day in life. Michael Frater will go on to be a track and field sprinter who specialized in the hundred meters' event. He won a silver medal at the 2005 World Championships and a gold medal at the 2003 Pan American Games for the event. I remember sitting home one day and watching the 2008 Olympics track and field and watching Michael Frater on the Jamaica 4x1 relay team beat the world record. He ran the second leg and the world saw him, Nesta Carter, Asafa Powell, and Usain Bolt make history by breaking the 4x1 record with 37 seconds at the time while attending Boyd H. Anderson

High School in Lauderdale Lakes, Florida! I didn't know Coach Bowden and Michael Frater would become who they are now, but I see how they approached school and sports. I understand now that the way you carry yourself and prepare your mind to be great can lead you to success.

To me, the only thing I was good at was socializing with people and debating sports. So, one day during lunch, I was roaming the halls and saw a diverse classroom of just kids talking with a teacher, so I just walked in! They all had a crazy look on their faces like can we help you? I was like yea, I just want to know what's going on in here? Being funny? One guy named Javier Martinez looked at me and said, "Yes, this is the Student Government Association. Are you here to enter your name to run for office?" I froze for a minute and was like yes, I would like to run for office! He explained to me that if I won, I would hold the position for the following year. He also said I would have to prepare a speech to present to the student body. So, I'm thinking to myself, what did I just walk into, but I was game. In my head, I was popular; I wasn't shy. I was handsome, and a lot of the student body would listen and relate to me! It's like it was meant for me to walk in a classroom, disturb it, and get away with it! I could only run for Treasurer because I didn't take the SGA class that present year. I was game, and I was confident! My competition was a junior, turning senior who was in advance classes called the IB (International Baccalaureate) program! She was very smart, but shy. We had to say our speeches at a pep rally. For the first time, I was a little nervous, but my speech promised everything. I remember saying I will try to bring Juvenile, an artist from Cash Money Records, who was the hottest rapper at the time to the school for a show! I stood up at that podium and felt real comfortable as people start cheering and clapping for me. I looked at all the candidates, and no disrespect to me, at the time, they didn't look like what the greater population of the student body look like. These individuals were in charge of making plans and decisions that would affect the entire student body. I got a standing ovation and a lot of students now knew my name and knew they had someone they could trust and believe in. They called it politics, and I looked at it as becoming popular! I felt real cool and calm after I was done and saw how the student body embraced and gravitated towards me. I have a develop a love for helping people over the years. I really felt after that speech that I could help change the face of Student Government by leading by example and not as a clown. I now had responsibilities, and teachers and students wanted to hold me accountable for all my actions. This is when I became a leader and started walking the talk!

I started to be stopped by students in the hallways who I never met who ask me questions and suggested ideas. I now had a responsibility to be a leader in school. I had a lot of people who voted for me and put trust in me to bring change! One day, a teacher, who I will leave nameless, but thank you my brother for everything, approached me. He said, "Paul Mompremier?" I said, yes. "Come to my class on your lunch break." I said, yes sir. He sat me down and asked me did I believe in God? I said, yes. He said, "Do you know who Allah is?" I said, no, then he popped in a VCR tape, and I watched it. It was a speech by the great and honorable Minster Farrakhan! Louis Farrakhan, Sr. is the leader of the religious group Nation of Islam. He served as the minister of major mosques in Boston and Harlem and was appointed by the longtime NOI leader, Elijah Muhammad, as the National Representative of the Nation of Islam. Farrakhan had on a red blazer and a black bow tie. He was passionate about what he was saying. He was speaking his truths and made sure people knew he meant business when he spoke. He was very intelligent and educated me from afar with black history and, still to this day, is a great role model for me. The classic line from that interview is when he told the host "You should be quite!" I wanted to be just like him and how he gave people hope and gave people the motivation to be great and spoke with so much passion. See, in high school, we were not allowed to discuss or teach religion in school. The teacher told me that he saw something special in me, and he believed I could become a young great leader with the Nation! I was honored, but I look at the teacher and was like yea, sign me up. What do I have to do? He gave me the basics, and I was deterred because I'm one of Haitian descent! I love Gyro and eating bacon. I would do a disservice not being 100% committed to the religion. He understood and wasn't too pushy, but I found myself realizing that I had a gift, and a lot of people were taking notice.

I remember joining a funded program called Project Dream by the Urban League of Broward County. Founded in 1975 as an affiliate of the National Urban League, the Urban League of Broward County is a community-based organization dedicated to empowering communities and changing lives in the areas of education, jobs, housing, and health. The program I was in" Project Dream" was led by a beautiful woman named Christine Bates. She was a great influence in my life. She told me stories where she marched for civil rights. She was spit on by white people for doing nothing. Her presence in a room was very strong, and I loved her like a mother. She took the time to make sure I knew that being a black young man has its disadvantages, but I could become something on earth. I remember watching the movie, Roots, and that's when I realized that I was surrounded by a lot of hate and evil, and you can't trust too many people A lot of people in the Urban League gave me hope and gave me a place to go after school that kept us away from crime with after school programs. It was a place that integrated with other high schools in the area like Dillard and Fort Lauderdale High School. I remember I was chosen to do a speech at Parkway Middle School, and they wanted me to be Malcom X. Malcolm X, born

Malcolm Little, and later also known as el-Hajj Malik el-Shabazz, was an African-American Muslim minister and human rights activist. To his admirers, he was a courageous advocate for the rights of blacks, and a man who indicted white America in the harshest terms for its crimes against black Americans; detractors accused him of preaching racism and violence. He has been called one of the greatest and most influential African-Americans in history. I had to create a speech to speak to the youth. They took me to many functions that empowered me to become a student involved with my community. They took me on a historic black college and universities tour. The Urban League of Broward County made me want to go to college and become someone influential in this nation. I remember going to wrestling practice and leaving early just to go to the Urban League. I was sought out by the drama department to partake in plays, and I would leave early to go to the Urban League. I found that was my getaway to a fun place that had real people who wanted me to become successful. The things I learn from my counselors there have groomed me and made me appreciate what our ancestors have done for us.

My senior year, I was well known by everyone: teachers, student body, coaches, principals, school officers, security, teachers, students of all ages, international students, IB students, and ESE students. I was known for being the loud outspoken, non-athletic, arrogant, nice kid to everyone. So, I ran for homecoming king. I didn't have a car, and I wasn't the captain of the football team, but I was popular for being positive! I ended up winning homecoming king because everyone voted for me. My homecoming queen was the beautiful red bone, Jackie Webley. I had a red girlfriend at the time, Jasmine Stokes, who I took for granted and broke up with because I was too big headed. I'm not going to lie; she was my heart, and the first girl I said, "I love you" to. I regret not going back with her because she was a great, beautiful person. I felt like I was the man on campus. I was still a virgin, but everybody thought I was getting the most tail cause every day I came to school smiling and profiling. I mean, you would've thought I was a young nature boy Rick Flair! I was a ladies' man. I always respected woman. My mother raised me right. Never put your hands-on women and always make them feel like queens. In school for the first time, there was going to be a Boy Pageant! Again, being competitive, I wanted to compete in that. The only thing I didn't know was that I was not going to do well in was the talent showcase. I can dress and put a nice outfit together. I was still selling candy! I was always dressed well. I can answer questions because I'm not shy in the public. But what would my talent be? I knew I loved music, and it inspired and motivated me, and I can dance. So, I had to go home and brain storm.

I went home and played music and role played songs and act it out. It was a song made by LiL Romeo, at the time Master P's son, "I don't need a Girlfriend," which caught my attention. Percy Robert Miller, known by his stage name, Master P, or his business name, P. Miller, is an American rapper, actor, entrepreneur, investor, author, filmmaker, record producer, philanthropist, and former basketball player. He is the founder of the record label No Limit Records, which was relaunched as New No Limit Records through Universal Records and Koch Records, then again as Gutter Music Entertainment, and finally, currently, No Limit Forever Records. He is the founder and CEO of P. Miller Enterprises, a conglomerate company, and Better Black Television, a cable television network. I was popular and my name started with a P, so it was only right that I do a song by his son. In vision, I knew exactly how the video was roller skaters, cheerleaders, signage, and a lot of energy. For me in a jersey with cheerleaders and roller skaters, man I was about to make a movie out of this talent show case. I knew people were going to sing, and I can't sing. I like to rap and loved rap music. So, long story short, I had a great performance. I made it to the last 3 finalists. It all came down to one question in the final question. Ms. Taylor and Coach Williams walked up to me, and asked me my final question. My question was "if you can put something in a time machine that can come back to Boyd Anderson, what will you put in it"? I thought about it. I said myself: To live again and enjoy high school and portray a positive example, so Boyd Anderson will always be in good hands. I won! The crowd went crazy and got crown again. So, I won homecoming king and now the crown—the first ever! Mr. Cobra, I felt like royalty. That's when I came up with the nickname "Prince." I felt like royalty, and I was a young man who held himself to a standard and gave myself respect first.

I got a one job in high school because my face became so known selling candy on the weekends. I one, day went in to Kentucky Fried Chicken, now known as KFC, for some honey barbeque wings. The manager thought I was fun and funny, so she offered me a job on the spot. I had no formal interview. She just asked me. Yea, you want to work here? I was like yeah! I fill out my application and just started working. It was fresh. I would work right in my neighborhood, and all I would do is fix food. I worked with a whole bunch of Zoë's that treated me like family. I used to burn my mouth eating so much food fresh off the grill. I gained weight, but the food was so good. I enjoyed working there, but this is a place where I would learn the importance of customer service and how important it is to satisfy customers. One day, it was my day off, and the manager called me and said she was short staffed. She asked me could I come in? I said, sure, no problem. I'll come right in. I got to work, and she told me to run the drive thru. I told her I never was trained to run the drive thru, but she insisted because that was the shift that need to be filled. I was energetic and ready to run the drive thru. I thought it would be fun and easy. Boy, was I wrong. I had to place the order, bag the order, handle the money, and then tell the customer "thank you." I was terrible at first, but got better in my eyes as the day went on. Then, I went home. No biggie, right? Wrong! I went in on a Wednesday, my day off, to go pickup my check because we got paid every week. The manager called me into her office, and she told me she must fire me! I was like, What? She said I got secret shopped by CHAMPS that day on drive thru, and the company decided to let me go because my score was very bad. So, I got fired on my day off, like Craig did on Friday! Craig in the classic Friday movie! Craig and Smokey are two guys in Los Angeles hanging out on their porch on a Friday afternoon, smoking, and looking for something to do. Encounters with neighbors and other friends over the course of the day and night, and their ensuing antics, make up the rest of the movie.

So, I'm about to graduate high school, and there was one more thing that I wanted. We had a graduation meeting with the senior class in our school auditorium to discuss how many tickets each student will get to give to family and friends. So, I came home, and I had an extra ticket. I told my mom that I want my father to come to my graduation. My mother sat me down and told me that the man that I thought my father was not my father. She called the guy that came to my house in Texas before we flew to Florida. She said that Garcia Desinor was my father. I was shocked crushed and all emotional. I felt betrayed. How can this man know me all this time and didn't acknowledge or checkup on me as his son? He had another family, and he was married when I was conceived. I have older brothers and sisters that I didn't know, and all this time, we were related. So, I felt like nothing, I started disrespecting my mom and hanging around the bad crowds. I didn't want to go to college anymore because I knew I would need my mom's signature and information. I didn't want her help or info because when applying for FASA (Florida Association of School Administrators) in Florida, they want to know how much money your parents made. I start rebelling and start disobeying T Will and my mom. Every other day, my mom was telling me to get out of her house. Then, I started to think again I was big and bad, and this is when Life hits.

CHAPTER 5 LIFE AFTER SCHOOL

So, I go from being a happy go lucky graduate to a depress kid that just ripped up a letter from Howard University! Howard University (HU or simply Howard) is a federally chartered, private, coeducational, nonsectarian, historically black university (HBCU) in Washington, DC. It is classified by the Carnegie Foundation as a research university with high research activity and is accredited by the Middle States Commission on Higher Education. To me, it would have been a great fit for me. I wanted to go there; most of my role models I met thru the Urban League encouraged me to go to a historically black university! So, after graduation, I just went and got a job to help my mother pay bills. I had to put school on the back burner to help my mom out. It was bad. I was getting up early in the morning to prepare breakfast and lunch at McDonalds! There were days when I would dread going to work, but I had no choice. As a young black teenager living with parents, it's always common to hear: You better go get a job or move out! I didn't have that silver spoon in which my parents were successful and wealthy and could pay for me to go to college. I didn't even have the grades to get full rides to all the colleges. I must take blame and ownership for myself as well. I didn't keep my grades up and do my homework. I went to school to socialize and just be a teen. It's like any kid that graduates from high school. I didn't have a plan or goals. I just went and did the minimum I had to do just to graduate. So, I found myself flipping burgers! I hated worked there. I remember sweeping and moping the lobby one morning. There was a group of old retired white men who came every morning and ordered the same thing: coffee and a sausage biscuit. On this day, one of the older gentleman looked at me and said, "Hey what's your name?" I said Paul. He said, "Paul you look like you not supposed to be doing this for the rest of your life." It was then when I just envision myself for a split second being an old man in this same McDonalds sweeping and cleaning tables in floors for the rest of my life. I had to do something different.

I was angry with my mom for a little while, but I must commend one man: Delroy Lindsey Sr! He was the father of my childhood friend, Delroy, Jr. He sat me down and had a deep conversation with me. He was heavy into church and told me the importance of respect and obeying thy mother and father. He taught me an important lesson, and I appreciated everything my mother did to raise me. See, I met Delroy, Sr. by always going to Delroy's house. Me, Darnell, Delroy, and my other brother, Marcus Hughes, were inseparable. We used to think we were the Hot Boys of Cash Money Records! The Hot Boys (often styled as Hot Boy$) is an American hip-hop group actively consisting of both past and present Cash Money Records rappers Lil Wayne,

Juvenile, B.G., and Turk. The original members of the group consisted rappers, Lil Wayne, B.G., Juvenile, and Turk. The Hot Boys made their first official appearance together on B.G.'s third studio album, It's All on U, Vol. 1. They soon released their debut album entitled, Get It How U Live! which sold over 300,000 copies, primarily in New Orleans. The album charted nationally as well at 37 on the Billboard R&B/Hip-Hop Albums Chart.

In 1998, Cash Money Records agreed to a 30 million pressing and distribution contract with Universal Records. This led to releases, such as Four-Hundred Degreez by Juvenile, which was certified four times platinum by the RIAA. The Hot Boys made numerous appearances on many of the albums' tracks, such as "Back That Azz Up" featuring Lil Wayne and Mannie Fresh, and "Ha", when the Hot Boys were featured in the music video. The album also contained a remix of "Ha" featuring the Hot Boys. The Hot Boys appeared on both Lil Wayne and B.G.'s albums in 1999, Tha Block Is Hot by Lil Wayne and Chopper City in The Ghetto by B.G. Both albums were certified platinum. The group also released singles, such as "Bling" and "Cash Money Is an Army" by B.G., "Tha Block Is Hot" and "Respect Us" by Lil Wayne, and "U Understand" and "I Got That Fire" by Juvenile. Darnell was LiL Wayne, Delroy was B.G, Marcus was Turk, and I was Juvenile! But just like the Hots Boys grew apart, so did we. Darnell end up moving to Georgia with his family. Marcus end up going to college at FAMU (Florida Agricultural & Mechanical University). Only Delroy and I were left in Lauderhill, but we grew apart. I still love them to this day and share a lot of memorable fun moments, but life goes on. We were literally going our separate ways just like the Hot Boys!

So now, I'm working at McDonalds early in the morning flipping burgers. I became prideful one day as times were getting hard and just quit McDonalds because they money wasn't enough. My mother was renting places only to get eviction notices when times were hard. When you a young adult and see that pink slip of you getting sued and owe someone money with that word EVICTION! big and bold, it makes your heart drop. I used to be ashamed of my house because it wasn't like my other friends' houses where there was a mom and dad in the house. Sometimes our power would be off, no food in the fridge, and I wouldn't be able to accommodate my friends in the same way that they accommodated me. Because I knew when I got home, the window would be cracked open, and I would sleep in pajama pants without a shirt because it would be so hot with no electricity! I felt like I was living in Haiti in South Florida. I don't want any sympathy for that time in my life because there are kids all over this nation that grow up in foster homes. They don't live with their parents for whatever reasons. Those kids sleep colder or hotter at night. It's kids that were just like me who didn't have food in the fridge or no lights in the house.

It was the norm for me in my neighborhood. I thought it was normal to go thru a little tough time here and there.

After high school, I started to realize my mom had bad luck in relationships. The men she invested in all cheated on her and left her broke financially and heart broken. I had to be her rock and have her back whenever she was down. I carried a lot of pressure on my back working full time and giving my mom money sometimes to help her pay rent. I saw my mom trade in a paid-off car that she bought cash brand new when my grandfather passed to make ends meet. My mom sacrificed so much to live in South Florida. I owe her a lot because she did whatever she had to do for me and her just to keep a roof over our heads. I ended up growing frustrated and leaving my mother's house just to sleep on my friends couches and room. My childhood friends, Delroy, Lander, and Kenny, let me live with them as I worked two jobs to keep money in my pockets. I told them throughout the years that I owe them forever for not allowing me to sleep on the streets and opening their homes to me. I'm forever grateful for them and their families! Then one day, I remember when I went to my old house to get clothes, and all the furniture was gone. My mother went and lived with her boyfriend at the time, Frank; my sister went and lived with her father Alex for a little bit, and I stayed at friend's house. I used to ride my bicycle up and down Shallow Side with a Blue Urban League book bag with no home to go to. I would just ride and see all the people in my neighborhood playing with each other, having family cook outs in their back yards, and see families walk in and out of their homes. It's painful riding around feeling alone. I had no way to get in contact with my mom or dad. I felt alone, and that's when I went into depression.

I end up bumping into one of my childhood friends and classmate, Marcus Caddette, when I was in the Broward Mall one day. We exchange numbers, and he ask me where I was living? I told him my friend, Kenny Royster, and I were looking for a place, so we could split the rent when his lease was up. He told me he had a place already with a room I could rent, and I would not have to buy a bed because there was a brand-new bed already there. I thought the price was low and affordable, so I took him up on his offer. I just received a raised in 2004 because the company I was working for at the time was just bought by an American sportswear and footwear retailer, operating in approximately 20 countries worldwide! I also just bought a '98 Honda Civic with my own money. Jumping off city buses with a $1,000 cash to put down on a car with any car lot that would give me a chance with no established credit. So, I did the math, and I could afford it. When I look back at it, the APR was 28% percent for a $,7000 car. I was robbed, but I paid it off, and it felt good. My credit was good for a while. I moved in with him and his girlfriend from high school, now his wife. It was an easy transition because I already had a great friendship with Marcus. We attend school together, attended Urban League of Broward County together, and his mother use to help me during high school. Some people don't have a great roommate experience, but to be honest, I never had one argument with Marcus and Melinda. Still to this day, we have a great relationship. I'm forever grateful for just bumping into Marcus that day at the mall.

Living in Deep Side Lauderhill as a young black man is an experience. My mom let me leave the nest, and I knew I would have to make decisions based on the environment I lived in. I would be lying if I sat up here and said I was always saying the right things and always made the best decisions. I messed up a lot in life. I ran the streets of Lauderhill with baggy clothes, gold teeth at times (pull outs), a gun my uncle help me pick out, and chasing tail! I was like a little part-time fake gangster. Living in Deep Side, women broke my heart, and I loved hard. So, when I was single, I just wanted to be a ladies' man. I never wanted to be in a relationship feeling down about another ex. So, I just stayed single. I feel a lot of men from the ages of 18 through 24 are not looking to get married and have kids! It happens, but I know it's not the ideal situation, so I have no regrets of things I did. I did everything to protect my life, family, and heart! Some days, I would get off work and come to my house and find it broken into. I was shocked when I found out who was breaking into my house to steal from me. May peace be upon them and their families. It never and still doesn't make sense to me that people steal from people who go out and work hard for the money. In that area, back in the day, it's always people walking around, sitting on corners hustling or shooting dice! Noisy young and old people gossiping and fighting outside. The pizza man won't deliver to your area because he got robbed. It was cool if you knew people, and people respect you. I would walk the streets of Lauderhill and get jumped by guys either to try to scare me or make their presence felt. So, I made sure I surrounded myself with people who could protect me. I hung with the OGs in the neighborhood. I looked up to the hottest rappers in my neighborhood at the time Solo and Ragu. I used to watch Solo, Ragu, and Silk just get respect everywhere they went. I was in a relationship with one of my exes whose big brother was well respected in my neighborhood! They were also my family—shout out to Trice, Travis, Wayne, and Vera Parker—I love you all for life. Trice was my love at one time in my life, and I call her O.J and my Ashanti. O.J because that's an inside joke we have, and Ashanti because to me that's her celeb twin. Wayne was a big brother to me and always made me laugh and gave me compliments. I used to get mad when I heard Wayne got in trouble with the law and got locked up for small things. Travis, aka Gulash, was a big brother that dropped jewels through his music and through conversations about the streets we walked and the people we had in our circle. Solo and Travis was and still is well known in Lauderdale because of their talents in music. Travis let me be in one of his rap videos a long time ago. They protected me from harm, and Vera cooked for me when I was hungry and treated me like her son all the time.

I was very flashy when I was on my own, so I can see why I was targeted. I used to walk around with the latest sneakers and the longest biggest chain I could waste my money on. I imagine some people would become jealous. I would go to night clubs in Fort Lauderdale and get into altercations with people because I didn't live in the city where I was having fun. The guy that liked the woman I was sleeping with was jealous because she wasn't dealing with him anymore, and he found out she was dealing with me. Silly things always had me guarded and cautious of where I went. But, back in the day, if you lived in Deep side Lauderhill, you weren't supposed to fear anybody else. That's where I get my demeanor from. I barely smiled because where I'm from and grew up, there are not that many things to smile about. At times, people from Deep side were noticeable because we had tattoos on our forearms or bodies and were known by five-five-one-nine. It stands for 55th Avenue and 19th Street! It's the central heart of Deepside! We ran from no one. We were raised to defend ourselves and never back down. There are hoods everywhere across the nation, and I'm not saying Deep side is the hardest or toughest, but it made me very strong. I got jumped there on the streets walking home by cowards. I fought a guy one on one and beat him up. He ran and told his friends that he got jumped by me and my friends. I guess it was their payback, but I walked away with no bruises. I still remember all the people involved and forgave them. Its apart of a young man's life in south Florida. Somebody is going to try you and disrespect you. You may have to knuckle up sometimes. As you get older, I encourage the youth from Broward County to walk away or have a conversation. Just don't kill each other. Thank God for friends who back some friends. When that happened, it lasted for about one minute until a car pulled up and said, "Paul is that you? He got back in that white car and pulled off.

It was times when I lived in Deepside that people would break into my house numerous times. Myself, Marcus, and Melinda would all work during the day, so nobody would be home. So, we would come back from work only to find our house door open or back door open. Sometimes, I would come home and my camcorder will be missing, homemade videos, and adult DVDs. I later found out that it was the maintenance. It was sad, and I told management but was mad that where you pay you rent, people don't have integrity. Then dudes from the neighborhood were breaking into our place. One time, some young kids from the way broke into my house. I knew they were young because I had a wall of shoes in my room. One robber took a pair of my shoes and left his shoes in my room. Talk about disrespectful, this was an ongoing issue. However, one day, I couldn't go home because our apartment section was roped off! My neighbor killed a robber who broke into his house. I was strapped at the time and use to carry my gun on my hip because in that area, getting robbed in broad daylight was normal. I never got robbed at gun point, but my mom did in the same neighborhood. I never got robbed, but they use to hit my house when no one was home. After a while Marcus, Melinda, and myself moved to North Lauderdale because we had had enough. I was happy we left. It was time to start a new chapter! That was the day I left Deepside. It would be a dream to have a street named after me, or even the over path since I lived on both sides. One day Paul one day that's a new goal!

CHAPTER 6 BABY MOMMA!

Growing up, I remember listening to LiL Boosie a lot. Torrence Hatch (born November 14, 1982), better known by his stage name Boosie Badazz, formerly Lil Boosie, is an American rapper and actor from Baton Rouge, Louisiana. Hatch was bestowed the nickname Boosie by his family, and he was raised in Southside Baton Rouge. As Boosie, he has released numerous regular studio albums while also contributing to a few mixtapes and compilations. He did a remix to a Young Jeezy song called "They Dykin." There was a line in that song that use to make me smile and get crunk! Two red bones kissing in the back seat! See at this point in my life, I grew an attraction for light skin women! I didn't discriminate, but if I look at a group of women, the red bone will get my attention. I used to sleep with girls, but was looking for a beautiful red girl along the way to settle down with. I used to always see this one girl, out of respect and my love for her and her family, I will leave nameless. She used to always carry herself like a lady. She was so sociable and loved by everyone she encountered.

I remember one year, I asked her to be my valentine, and she said yes. Boy, was I excited! I went out and bought a brand-new outfit to make a good first impression. I picked her up at her house and met her mom. Now, I was dressing kind of urban. Back then, Girbaud Jeans were very popular! First time I saw that brand of jeans was in high school. I saw a kid from New York wearing them, and I made fun of him. I was goofy and didn't know any better. He was like you down south people and up on fashion! They'll be down here soon. He was right because when I saw the Hot Boys wear them, I went and bought every color. Marithé Bachelorize and François Girbaud are French stylists, and in the late 1960s, they invented the industrialization of Stonewash. Baggy jeans were in style, and I had those on with a Girbaud red, button up to match and some clean, snow white and red Reeboks. I was clean, and nobody could tell me anything, except for her mother. I drove to her nice house to pick her up only to be told I should meet her mom. I wasn't scared of parents, but this lady was tough. I stood in her living room under a chandelier, and she drill me with questions. I stood tall and took all these questions because I'm old school—you must get along with the parents if you want to date the daughter. So, she has on my baggy jeans and baggy shirt, but let us go to dinner and the movies. I had a great time with her, but I think she was stuck on her ex-boyfriend. So, that's all it was: a date.

Time went by and I had an opportunity to go back with my high school sweetheart! We linked back up and everything was great until my family friends Shandra and Johnny Brooks invited me to a Christmas party. I went to the Christmas party and when I pulled up, the house looked familiar. I didn't recognize the house at all until I walked in the kitchen. There she was, my crush that was my valentine from back in the days! I was shocked, and she was looking at me like what you doing here? I told her who invited me and got my plate and walked off. Drinks were pouring, music was playing, and everybody was dancing and having a good time. So, I'm in the cut, and she goes dancing all over me. I was playing it cool because I knew she tried me back in the day and chose someone else. But we danced the night away and had a long conversation that night. So, as weeks went by, I end up deciding to role with the new, new situation and to not go back to my high school sweetheart, Jazz. So, that's going to be her nick name, NEW NEW, going forward in the book. She was fine as Laura London in the famous ATL movie! So, New New and I decided to go together and be in a relationship. Everything was pretty much great. She was the perfect girl for me. She had a little hood in her, she cooked, she was a clean person, and beautiful. We went on trips and a lot of outings, family outings, together. Her family embraced me and called me son-in-law for a while. I was in heaven, but then reality kicks in.

We had our share of disagreements. I would want to sometimes go hang out with my home boys, and she would play sick. Being the nice person I am, I would diss my friends to comfort her. She was my queen, my dream girl, so I didn't mind. Plus, the love making was amazing, so what's a guy to do? She started to become very needy. I figured, ok, everything is good, and the good outweigh the bad.

After a while, I decided that this was who I wanted to be with. I wanted New New to be the mother of my child. So, I start shooting her club up at least 3 times a week. We were rabbits anyway, and I'm blessed, so I knew she didn't mind either. But around that time, we started to argue more. She started to be controlling, and I remember we took a trip to Tampa for couples. We were having a good time enjoying each other's company. After love making and having conversations while taking shower, the topic of baby names came up. She looked at me and asked me what name I wanted to name our child if she got pregnant, and I pretty much said I would want a Junior! If it were a boy, I would want his name to be Paul Jeramiah Mompremier Jr. I gave it deep thought and wanted my son to have his own identity and name, but I wanted to continue the family legacy and name. So, I wanted to name him after my grandfather because he was the only father I had growing up. I thought of the name Jeremiah because it was cool and it start with J that was my ex's first initial in her name. The initials will be "P.J.," which will symbolize our unity and my last name. But if it were a girl, I wanted to name her Aaliyah Mompremier. I choose the name Aaliyah out of respect to the late great Aaliyah Dana Haughton, January 16, 1979, to August 25, 2001. She was an American singer, dancer, actress, and beautiful model. She was born in Brooklyn, New York, and raised in Detroit, Michigan. She was "Princess of R&B" and "Queen of Urban Pop." She was listed by Billboard as the 10th most successful female R&B artist of the past 25 years and the 27th most successful R&B artist in history. So, those were my ideas for names. On this night in Tampa while we are in the shower, my ex looked at me and asked if I liked the name of her ex-boyfriend!?!?!?! I said, "Wait, what??" My first reaction was to push her out of the damn shower, but I made a vow to myself to never put my hands on a woman. I thought it was disrespectful and hurtful. I left the room and came back but was never the same man after that night.

Everything started going downhill, and we started having problems. I couldn't look at New New the same anymore. The woman I fell in love with wasn't what she seemed. She started to miss my calls. I heard she was riding around in my Monte Carlo SS visiting other dudes. She had her friends lie to me about all her whereabouts. We would have full-blown arguments in front of family and friends. My jewelry started to go missing. My credit cards started to disappear and have charges on them. I pretty much said I'm not going to accuse her of anything, I'm just going to remove myself from this situation. So, one day I called her and said its time we break up. I went to her crib and got my belongings. It was ugly, but I couldn't take it anymore. So now I'm single and free. Then I got that call that would make any man's heart stop for two seconds. She called me and said she was pregnant! I forgot we took it there, and I was shooting her club up! It could've been the night we went out of town or a wild night at my place, but she was pregnant. So, with that big news coming through my phone, I calmly said, "Well, let's do this. I didn't want her to go through a pregnancy alone, and I knew I didn't have my father in my life. It was my time to step up be a man and make it work. So, I told her I would be there for her if we can communicate and get things right, then we can get back together and raise our family together. Nothing changed, there was a lot of arguing, and a lot of nights I didn't come to her house and rub her belly. I started to have doubts if she would change for the better. Around that time, Twitter was the new thing in July 2006! I used to go in on my ex because I was angry. I knew that she cared about me and checked on me every day. So, I gave her a show to watch. I was young and dumb and hurt her feelings. I was only hurting myself, my ex, and child and now raising her stress levels. I learned that hurting and posting negative comments about my personal life on social media is not a good look. The only people you are making fun of is yourself. Letting people in your business only makes things worst. I think all relationships that are going through hard times should communicate. Never go to bed angry; it will interrupt you from getting more sleep. Eventually, she blocked me from calling and texting her. I had no form of communication with New New! I was mad at myself because I brought it upon myself!

So eventually, I end up reaching out to her mother just to check up on her status and make sure New New was healthy and was eating. She told me that she would be at Coral Springs hospital one day before I went to work. So, without knowing where the doctor's office was, I got in the car and went looking for my baby and baby! I went on every floor, ran to every doctor's office, looking at sign in sheets. I hadn't seen or heard from New New, and now, she wasn't answering her phone. So, I finally found the office she was, but they wouldn't tell me about her medical condition or why she was being seen. They told me that they sent her to the hospital across the streets to get records. I ran over there. I ran into her and her grandfather, furious because I'm not going to lie, I don't get tired now, but I was exhausted then! So, I was mad when I saw her for not answering my calls or texts and not letting me know what's going on with the baby. So, I snatched her paperwork and medical papers and vacated the premises, jamming Young Jeezy Inspiration album, and with my foot on the gas, flooring it. I took the papers to a friend who I knew was in the medical field who could break it down for me. That was the day I was crushed! I found out that New New had to have an abortion because she had an ectopic pregnancy! I blamed myself and cried. I lost my what would've been my first born. I was just being young and dumb and not being responsible. Later that day, the police called my phone while I was at work and told me to return her medical records. I was mad that she gave the law my number, but I agreed to return her paperwork. The police asked me if I ran over any hospital police on bikes leaving the hospital, and I said, "No Ma'am." I left jamming Young Jeezy and didn't see any security on bikes LOL. I got off work and drove to New New's house and threw her paperwork all over the lawn. I was pissed that I had to find out that way.

I guess it wasn't my time to have kids, I wasn't ready, and I was too young. So, I had to just move on with my life. I thought that would be the last time I ever had to have an encounter with New New, but boy, was I wrong. So, we had a lot of mutual friends, and my friend, Lander, was expecting a baby girl: Khalani! So, they planned a nice baby shower! So, I haven't seen or heard from New New in months. My momma, Vita Roland, who took me in long time ago, met me outside and asked me had I seen New New? I told her, no. She looked at me and said that she was in there with a belly pad on! I was thinking there is no way she's got a belly pad, but she isn't pregnant? I couldn't believe it. Vita said that every time she stands up, her belly moves. The ones people wear in movies, the kind that they use in maternity stores? I texted my homeboy, Jason, and asked was she in there? He said, yeah! I asked with a belly? And he said, yeah. So, I walked in cool, calm, and collected. I saw her but didn't speak. I heard from other people that she was walking around with bathing towels and belly pads on around in the hood, but I never saw it. I knew she didn't live with her parents, so they didn't know either. But when I saw it for myself, I couldn't believe it. So, she stayed behind the table the whole day, and they played games. I won one game where a string to measure a prospective mother's stomach from the back. I got up and asked New New let me measure her belly in front of everybody, and she left. So, then, I thought that would be the last straw. I was wrong! I used to get my haircut from a family friend who was the best in Lauderdale, Micky Rallens—a shout out to Tru Heart and his movement. I heard she was having a baby shower. You know, in barbershops, men talk and they keep it real with one another and be honest. I told Micky that she wasn't pregnant and I would not attend any baby shower because there was no baby. I didn't get why would she would keep trying to continue this hurt. A lot of her family disliked me at the time, but at the end of the day, I was hurting, too.

So, after the dust settled, and no baby came, the lesson I learn from it was to keep people out of my business. Love conquers all! I reached out to New New before I wrote this chapter because we are now in a good place. She has a great job in Atlanta, she is a homeowner, and now is in love with someone else. She got the help and guidance she needed, and so have I. We have a great unique relationship now, and after all that drama, we can reminisce and roast each other of all the things we did to one another. I grew up as a man and had to own up for mistakes and the role I played in our relationship. The good outweighed the bad, and we are in a better place. As time passed, it healed our wounds. I'm not saying I'm perfect, but I know I'm at a better place when I leave things in my past! I will always have love for New New and her family for the rest of my life! Real Talk I'm glad I went through that. It made me slow down on having unprotected sex. My dream is to be a great father and great husband one day. It's going to take someone very special to fill that void. I love the journey of finding the right person. It may be hard sometimes, and nobody wants to be lonely or alone for the rest of his or her life. My advice is to just do the right thing by someone. If you don't have people's best interest at heart, don't waste their time! Love, Relationships, Marriage! All these things are beautiful, if done right!

CHAPTER 7 WORKING IN RETAIL

I am writing this chapter after a two-month delay. I had to find and seek approval to write this chapter. I wanted you all to know where I worked and share some of my destinations that help me become a man. To be safe, I will not mention where I'm currently employed. I wasn't raised with a sliver spoon. My parents didn't have the money to send me to college. I was forced to make money and earn anything I ever wanted. One thing I learned is that when you work for somebody, you follow their policies and procedures. When you are your own boss, you answer to no one, but you work harder to get money! So, as I write I will have the energy of Nas as he wrote the Classic diss record against Jay-Z "Ether." Nasir bin Olu Dara Jones, better known by his stage name, Nas, is an American hip hop recording artist, record producer, actor, and entrepreneur. The son of jazz musician, Olu Dara, Nas has released eight consecutive platinum and multi-platinum albums, and has sold over 20 million records worldwide since 1994. Jay Z is an American rapper, entrepreneur, and investor. He is one of the most financially successful hip hop artists in America. In 2014, Forbes estimated Jay Z's net worth at nearly $520 million. He is one of the world's best-selling artists of all time, having sold more than 100 million records while receiving 21 Grammy Awards for his musical work and numerous additional nominations. I love what I do, and to be honest, giving over 14 years of my life to retail has help me become the man that I am today.

It all started one day when I was home and my friends, Delroy and Darnell, came to my house and ask me if I wanted to go look for a job with them at the Sawgrass Mall. I was listening to Nas album Stillmatic, a classic, while playing John Madden Football on PlayStation. I didn't want to go because the album was jamming and Nas is the reason why I start listening to up-north music in the first place. I was a down-south type of fan when it came to music. So, I was in my zone, but figured I would tag along with Darnell and Delroy to the Sawgrass Mall. We went and walked that whole mall in every store and asked for applications to fill out and asked if they were hiring. Back in those days, you had to do the ground work; there were no applications online. You had to go in with professional clothes and introduce yourself and meet with managers. It's all up to that one first impression. I was a very sociable person and never was the shy type. We walked into the Reebok store in the Oasis part of the mall and asked to talk to the manager. Right then and there, we went outside filled out our applications and met a man named Rudy.

Rudy was a manager for the Reebok store and was very serious. So, we sat in a circle and he drilled us with questions and told us if we got the job, he would contact us. I wanted to work there because at that time, Reeboks was the cool shoe to have. The Reebok Classics was the first-day-of-school shoe. All black, all white, and navy Club C's were a favorite of mind. The Reebok Mid, the Allen Iverson Questions, the comfortable Reebok's with the air DMX cushion technology, and the lists goes on. So, I really wanted to work there just because of my love for sneakers. We left the store and continued to apply at more stores we liked and went home back on the city bus. The next week, Rudy, the manager, called the house phone and told me he would like to offer me a part-time job. I was happy. I called Delroy and Darnell to ask if they got a call, too, but they didn't. I told them I had accepted the job and would be starting the job. I did want all of us to work there, but they only picked me.

Working for and at Reebok was a great experience for me. I was into the shoes we sold, and I always liked helping people. After working long hours during the week, it started to affect my grades while in high school. I would get off at about 10:30 p.m., then catch the last bus home to walk at night home in the dark the streets of Lauderhill. So besides sitting next to homeless people on the bus, who will ride the 72 route all day, and having to sit next to people who smelled like a whopper, only to go sleep on the bus and be tired. I started to get smart and learned how to block out people I didn't want to hold a conversation with. I would buy a CD player with headphones and listen to music, so people wouldn't talk to me. Then, I bought a bike, so I could get home faster after work. So, I ended up quitting before Reebok fired me because it just wasn't working with school.

So, I'm jobless again and I found myself shopping and playing basketball at Just for Feet Sawgrass Mall! Just for Feet Inc. was an athletic shoe and sportswear headquartered in Birmingham, Alabama, which became one of the largest and fastest growing athletic stores in the United States. In 2000, Footstar acquired Just for Feet. It closed its last store in 2004. I had a friend from Boyd Anderson name kurt and the manager, named Trish Nelson, who inspired me to fill out an application to worked there. Again, I was faced with a first impression interview face to face, and I passed. I didn't know what people saw in me, except for a respectful young man that likes people and like to smile. I got another chance to sell shoes, and they also had a reward program for selling Reeboks. It was the perfect place for me to work: they had music, free popcorn, a basketball court, and they sold every sneaker brand there. I met great people when I worked there that I can share stories about a few. I started off as a part-time sales associate that just did stock in the backroom. Then, it became busy, and they needed help on the floor. I was trained to learn and understand the importance and reason the shoes are put in order and make sure everything was in place. So, I knew where everything was and didn't talk to some of the associates or shift leaders. So, when my number was called, I went out and balled out. I became a sales associate and left the stock room.

I built confidence and started to think I was the best sales rep until we got a new manager to the team. My store was a great place to work, but I learned there that people steal internally as well. We had a new Nelson to our store, and his name was David Nelson. He was a great, strong, serious manager. He was a fan of the Godfather movie and always acted like he was one of those men. So, he had an ego, and I had one. So, one day he walks up to me and said, "Paul, you ever sold an insole? Or shoe cleaner?" And I got defensive real quick and said, "Man, people don't want to buy that stuff." He then he asked if I even try to show it? I gave every excuse in the book, but that's where I learned the importance of discipline, effort, and having tough conversations. David Nelson looked at me told me if I can't sell the other things besides shoes, I can't work there. He broke it down and said I was not doing anything but putting my name on a box I grabbed. He said I was not a salesman. What else could I sell that's not easy? They come in already looking for shoes. Can you make people looking for shoes buy something else they didn't plan on buying? At the time, I was going thru financial struggles, so I needed to keep this job because I was never being a fan of looking for another job. So, I took on his challenge and started to sell accessories and took that one conversation we had and kept it with me in my career. I know at times, people who worked with me on my teams probably said, "Paul is too hard on us; he always is strict." I learned from David Nelson in that moment to dig deep. Stop taking pride in doing something easy, challenge myself, and try to be the best at every aspect of the business. I was feeling myself so much that David Nelson created a monster. Now, not only could nobody out sell me, now I could say nobody could sell more cleaners, protectors, and insoles than me. I learned that to run any team or staff, there needs to be a leader, such as that father who walks around and tightens up everything. There needs to be a disciplinarian, not your friend or brother. That's the way I conduct myself every day at work and would lead by example. David Nelson said he was bringing one of his boys to come and outsell me one day. His name was James Brooks. James was good; he was another young hustler from Miami. He is now a friend of mind along with a group of other guys we work with. We had a new store manager named Ishaq Ali (Ish), who is still a good friend to me and still gives me good advice to this day. Ish went on to be one of the best managers I ever seen from a far. He got promoted to a store in the Pembroke Lakes Mall and did numbers. I remember Ish taking me out on the town showing what the Miami night life was about. Sometimes Ish works part time side by side with my good barber, Jason, who keeps my Boosie Fade on point! Shout out to Platinum Style Kutz and Nelson Franqui where I go to have good conversations and a good cut!

See, I wasn't a fan favorite when it came to the staff and crew that work there. David Nelson made me feel like a superstar, and it made other associates step their game up. His way of producing sales results worked because he made his staff compete. I use his approach now some days with my team. Some of the shift leaders that worked 40 hours couldn't out sell me. They had clicks in my store. Some of the staff was dating and I didn't know; I stayed to myself because I was from Lauderhill. We had people from Sunrise, Parkway, and Miami! So, for a while, we were to ourselves, and now, we were more like a team. Management caught and fired the people who were stealing. So, we had a good group of people. I knew the riff was over it one day. My ex, Trice, dropped me off at work, and I was getting out the car feeling myself taking my time. People were honking at me, telling me to hurry up. I stepped out and wiped myself down, taking my time. I thought I was good looking, the best seller, and I felt a Prince couldn't be rushed into work. Man, some dudes jumped out the car, and for a split second, they tried to rush me. All I saw was Billy (BJ) Parrish come to my rescue. He flew out the store and said some words I can't repeat and came to my rescue. I think when he did that, all the tension in the store came to an end. I'm still cool with all those dudes: Damian, Gert, Fritz, Orville, David, Andrea, and Rick! My relationship with BJ has come full circle. BJ was a funny guy who could make anybody laugh. I just recently saw him while I was writing this book and prayed for him because he has been in and out the hospital.

Then, I was offered a promotion to assistant manager for Footaction inside the Sawgrass Mall. It didn't happen right away, but David and Trish trained me good until the time came. I will forever be thankful to Just for Feet or the people who started Footstar because they introduce me to retail. Foot Locker bought Footaction in 2004, and Just Feet closed. So, if Trish Nelson, David Nelson, and Sandy Beeson would've never promoted me out of Just for Feet, I would've been looking for a job again. Foot Locker Retail, Inc. is an American sportswear and footwear retailer with its headquarters in Midtown Manhattan, New York City, and operates in approximately 20 countries worldwide. I started there with one manager, and she was transferred, and there was a new manager who came to work there. So, it was a change, but I change and adapt easily if everything goes right. I went through a lot of growing pains. At Foot Locker, I learned how to work long hours and preserve my energy when trying to make it through an all-day shift during holiday season. I have worked with a lot of great people while working there.

First person I met was a man named Tony Turturici, and he was my future district manager. I walked into Foot Locker not knowing who he was while employed with Footstar and just asked him how much do they pay assistant managers. He was in Coral Square Mall cutting open a box, and I just ran up on him. The crazy thing is, I remember the manager who ran that store at the time was Steve Dewesee, who eventually would be the man who was responsible later in my career for helping me. He basically didn't tell me any money figures but told me it would be a great opportunity for both banners. The relationship Tony and I have is great because he met me when I was young, and we have had plenty of conversations. I respect him because he gave me chances when I messed up. He has probably the longest tenure of anyone I met in this company. I met my first manager who was a young, hungry, cocky Erik Conway. He and I are the same sign, and he was always hungry for more. He wanted to own Foot Locker in my eyes when I first met him. He was my current district manager, but recently put in his two-weeks' notice to become a cop. Erik and I have a great respect for one another, but at a time like this, I don't understand why anyone would want to be a cop. I wished him well and prayed that he would be safe. I owe a lot of credit to another man I will mention later who encourage me to have a sit-down conversation with Erik later in my career to work with him gain to build a district Erik was promoted to. I saw him become a father over the years and mature and give me the game. I knew we good at getting along because we share a favorite player, in Kobe Bryant. Kobe Bean Bryant is an American retired professional basketball player and businessman. He played his entire 20-year career with the Los Angeles Lakers of the National Basketball Association. He entered the NBA directly from high school and won five NBA championships with the Lakers. Bryant is an 18-time All-Star, 15-time member of the All-NBA Team, and 12-time member of the All-Defensive team. He led the NBA in scoring during two seasons and ranks third on both the league's all-time regular season scoring and all-time postseason scoring lists. He holds the NBA record for the most seasons playing with one franchise for an entire career. Kobe Bryant's mindset, the way he approaches games, and business is what inspired me to be just like him. He doesn't care who doesn't like him, when he competes he only wants to win and be successful. That's the attitude I have every day moving up in the company sometimes. I just want to do my job, inspire people, and earn the respect of all my coworkers above and under me. I remember when I talked to him one day about creating a brand to help the younger generation and motivate people. He believed in me and saw my vision. He even bought one of the first batch of shirts I ever printed—big shout out to Erik Conway. To me Erik was like a great used car salesman, but one thing I will respect is he takes pride in being a father. Me and Erik share the same upbringing, growing up without guidance.

I was transferred to many stores after that because assistant managers were never going to sit long in one store in the district I was working in. That's why a lot of people in Broward County know me. The company let me work in different cities and malls. I remember meeting Reece Bentley and Terrance Brooks, the first black district managers I ever saw while employed with Foot Locker, who gave me encouragement that I could move up in this company. I met them while working for the legendary Steve Dewesee at Broward Mall. Steve was an old-school manager who I believe was my last hope to teach me how to be a manager. I believe everybody washed their hands with me because they never met someone like me! I was hard to deal with because I felt I was the best, but I had to prove myself at every store I worked at. I worked with integrity and the competitive edge that David Nelson trained me to have. While working there, I got news that David Nelson passed away doing a bank drop! He was shot and robbed for money and didn't make it home to his family. It broke me because he was a great friend, and mentor. I worked with great people at Broward Mall that's now called Westfield Mall. One of my favorite coworkers of all time is Elaine Johnson. We would crack and joke on customers all the time and never played with people who tried to steal or get over. She is like a big sister to me and a great active mother. Irvin Valkowitz is also one of my favorites. He is a little older than me, but he was a fun guy to work with. I think he and I alone gave Steve most of his grey hairs. I mimic my style from a great manager name Jason. He was a sharp manager, that wouldn't break a company policy if you paid him. That's who I want to be like, Jason won every award, and was a manager trainer, then promoted to district manager. So, who would be my next mentor?

It was news that a guy from New York named Toney Irvin was going to take over the Foot Locker on Broward Blvd and 441. He was a manager trainer, and took over a store in a poor neighborhood and, with hard work, make it one of the best in the company. Steve told me that he wanted to talk to me. I didn't know why, but I'll entertain it. So, he came, and we sat outside the mall and talked, and it was a conversation that I will always remember and cherish. It pretty much was a conversation about growing in the company and asking me what was stopping me. At that point in my life, I was content; I didn't want more out of life. I was cool. I had my own place, my own car, jewelry, and made the same amount of money that managers made. One thing that he made me realize was that I wasn't making his amount of money, and he was a manager. He told me that if I moved, there was good money to be made. I could get more out of life. I didn't always agree with everything he taught me, but I appreciated him because he always kept his door open for me when I needed someone to vent to and trusted that it would stay between him and me. Toney Irvin as a manager trainer taught me I was only as good as the people I produced. I took that message and ran with it.

Two of my former part-time associates made me the proudest. One was a kid named Luis Sanchez; he was my part timer who worked with me at a tough mall in Miami: 163rd Street Mall. I ended up transferring him to Orlando. I called Terrance Brooks and told him to give him a shot. Luis ended up becoming a manager and won an award I never received, Rookie of the Year! You only get one chance at Rookie Manager of the Year! I went to work every day, working hard so I can win Rookie Manager of the Year and never got it. Another individual I want to share is my old cashier, Jennifer Laurent. Jennifer Laurent also worked with me at 163rd Street Mall. When I interviewed her, she told me that her manager at Champs didn't want to train or promote her. He told her if she wanted to be promoted, go climb that ladder over there. I gave her a chance because the staff needed a complete make over. She helped year after year, and I promoted her until I ended up leaving the store. Jennifer also won an award I never won, Manager of the Year, in the same year Luis won his award. It's crazy and rare that a Manager Trainer, Rookie Manager of the Year, and Manager of the Year, all come out of a small KFL store in 163rd Street Mall in North Miami, Florida. There are many associates that worked with me that I'm proud of from Rosa Hobson, Damian Kerr, Andrew Jean-Boutin, etc. So, I guess Toney Irvin I can say I made you proud, my people speak for me. He was one of the best manager trainers I have ever come across and still is my friend until this day. He is no longer with the company. So, who would be my next mentor?

We got the word that our Regional Vice President was about to change. It was at an award meeting when I first met him for the first time. His name was George Jenkins. George Jenkins was an African-American man who had a great track record with the company. He brought new energy and made sure that everyone understood he wasn't here to lose. He made sure that he visited every store and let everyone believe if anyone were here to grow and win, he wanted that person on his team. I remember he use the word "fluff" in his speech to describe people who were here for the wrong reasons. He was the truth. I never met someone who could motivate people to get better. I see why he was our new leader because he would do a visit and take off his blazer and help us work. George Jenkins to me is like the Ray Lewis of retail. George and I grew a relationship that started with respect and results. I told him if the opportunities came, I would work hard. He, too, made sure he was available when I had any issues. I always kept it real with him. I made sure when a promotion came, my name had to be in the discussion. People like Todd Brown and Doyle Logue always made sure people said Prince is the real thing and deserved a chance. Todd was a down to earth father figure to me as well. He did numbers in Florida Mall Orlando and work his tail off to get promoted as well. Todd is guaranteed to make anyone laugh and smile. I love that dude, and will always have his back. I was never an ass kisser. I just made sure on any shift in any store no one would out work me. Doyle Logue, I met him at Lauderhill Mall. I remember I had the Nextel that "Chirp Chirped" and had some Tony Montana ringtone going off. Doyle was a mean investigator, but I don't steal so he never gave me any pressure. Doyle impressed me because of his loyalty to his coworkers, and loyalty to his family and wife. Doyle is another man I respect and want to be like one day. George Jenkins was promoted to a big position in the New York Office, and Todd Brown has been promoted to Regional Vice President. Doyle Logue is still with the company close to retirement, but I love them to death and glad we cross paths because they are key reasons why I would never walk away from the company. Meeting older men like this was very key to most of my success because at times, I would want to get another job. I know these father figures invested their time and energy to make sure I succeeded, so I never let them down. They were all father figures, and I'm thankful they took time out to just give me the game and make me a better professional. Now some days I'm consider the "OG" I'm the one people trust to call before the do something or need advice.

I worked with a lot of great people, and I can't put them all in my book, or the book will go on forever. I also have hired a lot of great people, and some may have left the company or are still with the company. I met very close friends working for the company: James Monde, Corey Johns, Anson Bouie, Jacquelyn Vaz, Chantale Ghazi, and Giatree Sighn! These are people still there until this day no matter what and will help me and tell me when I'm wrong. They motivate me to do better and keep pressing on. Sometimes, there were times when I wanted to quit and give up, but these individuals helped me. I worked in plenty of different malls in plenty of different cities. I ran across the poorest lady who couldn't afford the shoes her son wanted. I've helped the rich and rude when I overheard a lady tell an associate, "Go fetch my shoes." I received death threats because someone didn't get to purchase a pair of Jordan's. I just recently had the Space Jam Jordan release come out and a black lady ran up on me at my store and asked why was I checking names and ID for sneakers. I'm sure she wanted the Jordan's, too, so I told her for the Christmas Jordan's. She pulled out her police badge like that would scare me and said, "Oh, I can't just come in and shop?" I said sure, go ahead. She walked in for less than 20 seconds and walked right out and said to me, "I hate Black People." In my mind, I thought racism still exists, and it can be from your own kind at times. In my mind, I thought why on earth is she a cop, and why are my tax dollars being used to pay people like her to protect and serve?

I also learned that people will do anything to buy shoes. When LeBron James brought his talents to South Beach, I was promoted to a store that would carry most of his exclusive sneakers. People would sleep outside for a whole week to get the shoes. People would try to bribe me and offer to buy me lunch just to get their hands-on shoes, all so they can re-sell them. I knew of some people that would fall victim to the bribe and didn't have the integrity to do things the right way, but that's not me. See, when I clocked in for work, I worked for Foot Locker; I didn't work for sneaker heads. You can't buy me with money and then if I were dumb enough to lose my job for hooking up someone, and then I would be out of a job. That couldn't happen, and I wasn't in position to do that. Around that time, my mother was jobless and my sister was jobless. I got a promotion but was still living from check to check. I had great times at that store. I got a chance to meet NBA players LeBron James, Dwayne Wade, Dwayne Wade, Sr., his father, who is a regular shopper at the mall where I work at now. DJ Khaled, professionally known as DJ Khaled, is an American record producer, radio personality, DJ, and record label executive. Also, there was Tim Hardaway, Glen Rice, the boxer Lennox Lewis, the motivator Howard H. White who gave a speech who inspired me when I was going thru a rough time and gave me his book "Believe to Achieve"!

I thought long and hard to share stories and obstacles with you all that I went through that made me strong. I can go on for days, but we will save that for another time. There were people that wanted me to quit, treated me unfairly, and are shocked that now that I am a trainer with the company now. I must thank Erik Conway and Aaron Flamand, my new Regional Vice President, for giving me the chance. My encounters with negative people help me to become the great manager/trainer I am today. They couldn't break me; I'm still strong. One of my favorite quotes is from the movie Antwone Fisher. Antwone Quenton Fisher is an American director, screenwriter, author, and film producer. His 2001 autobiographical book, Finding Fish, was a New York Times Best Seller. The 2002 film, Antwone Fisher, was written by Fisher and directed by Denzel Washington. I didn't let black balls take my eye off the prize. I didn't let awards validate me, I stuck with my work ethic and core values. I knew once people didn't have no more kissing up to do, they must outwork me and compete. There are a lot of people who cosign me, so I must deliver. I must lead by example, and I got that from watching Invictus. When Mandela asked, "What's your philosophy on Leadership?" It made me a better manager! The film tells the inspiring true story of how Nelson Mandela joined forces with the captain of South Africa's rugby team to help unite their country. Newly elected President Mandela knew his nation remained racially and economically divided in the wake of apartheid. Believing he could bring his people together through the universal language of sports, Mandela rallied South Africa's underdog rugby team as they made an unlikely run to the 1995 World Cup Championship match. As I'm writing this, South Africa runner Wayde van Niekerk is a South African track and field sprinter who just broke the world record for 400 meters at the Rio 2016 Olympics!

Retail has been my longest relationship, and I'm glad I am blessed to work with great people and a great company like Foot Locker Inc. This year, I had the opportunity to talk and meet some of my company's top elite executives. They came and asked questions about how do I produce so much numbers and beat all these beautiful stores, all in this small box? At first I was honored because at times, in my career, my work ethic went unnoticed. It was simple. All praises go to my team that surrounds me because working with me is a very tough task. I love and respect all my employees, and I demand that they always give me their best effort. Second, I'm a seasoned veteran in the game. I have had many success stories, have a lot of wisdom, overcame a lot of obstacles, and defeated adversity. Third, my pain motivated me to be nothing less than great. I was always overlooked because people with power would lie to me to make themselves look good and hold my career back that was destined for greatness. I'm very strict, and like to keep a clean, well-organized store 24/7. So, we go on and on about visuals and merchandise, what sells and what doesn't. As I'm talking, there are no worries, I'm not afraid of voicing the truth or shy away from anything. So, both groups gather their things and say they will stay in touch and wish me well for this next upcoming year! My staff that were there were all smiles as I congratulated them. There is no big secret; when we are at work, we are getting paid. I'm bothered when I go places, and people act like the company owes them something. It's people who go to work and feel like someone should be glad they even showed up. It's people applying for jobs every day that have extreme work ethics and need that one more shot. My secret to success is I WORK HARD! I was that kid that had no place to sleep. I was that kid whose house used to be broken into. I was that kid who had the fake Jordan's. I was that kid in debt eating ramen noodles and cereal everyday as an adult because I made poor decisions with my money. If I'm the highest paid employee in my store, everyone in my store should know why. I don't have to work and sweat so hard that I leave work smelling like a whopper. I must lead by example and show the next generation and the future that you can never question the person in charge. I have built a reputation and legacy that can put me up against anyone in the company, and say I'll, put Paul MOMPREMIER in there and change will come! They left and gave me a few heads-up about some possible addition that's coming to South Florida. So, yesterday was a great day. I didn't get promoted or anything, but I know when those guys left, they knew who the truth is. Work hard, people. People may not notice on the first or second go around or give you praise, acknowledgement, or a pat you on the back, but I'm here to tell you, if you work hard, your blessings will come!

The customers and families that continue to shop and follow me from store to store are amazing. Retail has taught me to be a man. I didn't have a father figure growing up, so the mentors I had taught me about life and how to deal with different personalities. Working in retail is where I met some of the women in my life. That's where my former cashiers Jackie and Chantale became my only female friends until this day. To make sure, they gave me the female advice I needed to make good decisions, and I continue to treat woman the way they are supposed to be treated. Glad I worked in retail. I know have a new district manager in Jefferson Moore. He probably won't think I will put him in my book, but I have been a fan of his from a distance. He is a real and honest district manager. He puts his faith, family, and people he works with first. He is always even keel. I don't ever have to think, ok, is he playing me, or have any ulterior motives when he talks to me? He is a blessing to work with, and he is helping me become a better professional as well.

CHAPTER 8 DON'T SHOOT!

On April 21, 2011, my life change forever. It was my day off and I was chilling with friends in my old neighborhood, Deepside Lauderhill. At that time, it was getting better, but at the time, I couldn't put a face to all my enemies. I grew paranoid, hanging on corners with some friends, I didn't know if they were my friends, so I carried a gun on me always. On this day, on the way home, I wanted to go see my mentor, Toney Irvin, who at that time was the general manager at Aventura Mall for the company we work for. We had a big Reebok Flex shoe program going on, and all my part timers took all our shirts. My store needed more, so my mentor, Toney said to come and get some. So, I pulled up to the mall a little turned up. Jamming Young Jeezy! Jay Wayne Jenkins, better known by his stage name Young Jeezy (or simply Jeezy), is an American rapper from Atlanta, Georgia. In 1998, he launched the label imprint CTE World (then known as Corporate Thugz Entertainment). One thing that Young Jeezy and I have in common is that he was supposed to have an older brother, just like me who was supposed to be born before him, just like me. Living in poverty-strict environments, a father figure or older brother or some male influences are needed for guidance. So just like Jeezy, I lived thru music! Music makes me feel good. Some people hear loud noise, but to me, hip hop is like my gospel. Sometimes, I just apply whatever message I hear through songs to my life to motivate me to get through whatever I need to get through. Probably, he was one of the most inspirational artist I was blessed to hear.

So, I pulled up in my black and silver Monte Carlo SS, bumping my music loud. I parked and got out of the car, turn on my alarm and walked in the entrance by the Paul restaurant that is closest to where I had to go. I walked into the mall and went straight to the store to pick up the shirts and leave. As I'm walking out the mall, I saw one policer officer walk by me, who was entering the mall with a big gun. I walked past like, dang, he looked like he was about to shoot the heck out of somebody! I walked out the mall, and I saw literally 10 cop cars and a whole bunch of officers with their guns out yelling, "Get on the Ground!" I start walking fast towards my car like, boy, I've got to get up out of here. It's about to go down. Then I heard, you get on the ground now! I remember I had on an "I am African" shirt and some Jordan Spizikes! So, I got on the ground, and the police searched me and found my gun! Why didn't I leave the gun in the car? I don't know? So of course, I'm on the ground like what I do. One cop was telling me to shut up; they were taking me to jail. I told them I had a license to carry. Then one cop asked, "You tried to shoot a lady and her daughter in the parking lot? I looked at him like Russell Westbrook gave the reporter after asking a dumb question. So, they weren't hearing me, and I gave up. I had to go to jail. So, they booked me in Miami. First thing I thought of was I don't want to lose my job, and I don't want to scare my momma. So, I know like in the movies, when you go to jail, you get one call. I told the police officer to get my District Manager's number out my phone and the numbers of two managers I worked with at the time. He was nice and did that for me. So, I called all of them, and my district manager and mentor were the only ones sending messages through my floor superior. I made my calls, then they booked me. I know I was a little out of shape, but they listed me at 6'1 and weight at 210, brown eyes, and black hair; they got some right and some wrong. In my mug shot, I was emotionless. So many thoughts ran thru my mind. I asked what I was being charged with? The charge was aggravated assault; a felony that could've resulted into 5 to 10 years in prison.

I stayed in the holding cell, and then went to my floor where I would be for the next 2 days. The first day, I slept in the cell. I was so angry; how can I be locked up because of a lie a lady told. I was mad that I even went to that mall, second guessing doing favors for my store. Then, I was paranoid because I didn't want to get bullied or communicate with any of the other dudes who were locked up. I didn't want to eat because I heard stories about how inmates peed and spit in food. I woke up the next day to go see the satellite judge who would order to have me released. They held me for another day to be jerks; I guess the longer you stay in there, the more money the city makes. The second day, I was just sitting and thinking to myself, I do not want to ever be here again. Maybe it was a sign from God to show me that if I don't straighten up, this is where I could be. After having that time to think about everything, I knew I had to be different and stop walking around with my gun.

They took my gun from me, so while I was on probation until my court date, I didn't have that gun. I had time to see if I could live and walk around without it. I had to stop hanging around people I didn't trust. I was let out by 11:50, so I caught a taxi home and went to work the very next day. The people that I called while I was in there acted like they were shocked to see me. I knew then who was for me and against me. Before I went to work, I stop by Five Guys to get a big bacon cheeseburger. I was real hungry. I sat in the back and devoured my meal! My staff didn't know what happen, but I did. I just helped customers and went about my day. I made sure that moving forward, I had to make sure I knew the days to check in with the state representative. As I waited for my court date to go before the judge while out on bond, I had to stay out of trouble and not get into any run-ins with the law. I had to tell my mom about everything just in case I lost my case. She was more relieved that I didn't call her while in there. She worries about me a lot. I didn't want to scare her. I got that call from the state and they tried to persuade me to take a plea deal, so I wouldn't do the same amount of time. I was on the phone with them, and I told them they can keep that deal. I GOT FAITH, and you all don't have a case and hung up on them. I hung up the phone mad. I prayed heavy the day before my trial and even told God. I know I'm not saved, and I feel bad asking you to help when I know I don't pray daily. But I promised to talk to him more and move a lot differently.

The day of my trial, I remember driving to court with the music low and talking to my district manager, mentor, and mom. I parked my car, walked into the court house, and I sat and waited. I grabbed my chain, said a prayer, did my Catholic kiss to the top of my forehead across the body, and put the charm back in my shirt. As I waited, I saw a lady look at me, pray, and leave the court room. They called me up; the judge looked at the state and asked if they had a witness; they said no, and my case got dismiss! PRAISE GOD!! I was beyond ecstatic I walked in that court room with no public defender or plea deal, just me and GOD, and we won! The judge ordered my ban from Aventura Mall to be lifted because I work in retail and could possibly work there one day if a promotion came. She also ordered that I get my gun back. I walked out of that court room smiling. As I was leaving, the cop who arrested me told me I was lucky! I laughed at the racist bastard and said, "Excuse me," and primetime stepped right out that court room. I knew then that I was put on earth for a reason, and there was a God! I got a lot of hassle picking up my gun from the Aventura police department. They mean mugged me, said little petty things, trying to provoke me. I knew now that I couldn't let words or people trick me out of my position. A lot of people know that if they are something to you, they can get a reaction out of you. I'm here to tell you, the strongest individuals are the people who have self-control and who are not easily influenced. When I first started this chapter, I wanted to make it about how I fell in love again. During my thought process of Prince Motivation as a brand name and a motivational company, I was in a relationship. It came to an end, and a bigger issue came to surface that I needed to address. I think police brutality is at an all-time high. The first time I ever heard about it was when I heard about Emmett Till. Emmett Louis Till was an African-American teenager who was lynched in Mississippi at the age of 14 after reportedly flirting with a white woman.

Till was from Chicago, Illinois, visiting relatives in Money, a small town in the Mississippi Delta region. He spoke to 20-year-old Carolyn Bryant, the married proprietor of a small grocery store there. Several nights later, Bryant's husband Roy and his half-brother, J. W. Milam, went to Till's great-uncle's house and abducted the boy. They took him away and beat and mutilated him before shooting him and sinking his body in the Tallahatchie River. Three days later, Till's body was discovered and retrieved from the river.

Till's body was returned to Chicago. His mother, who had mostly raised him, insisted on a public funeral service with an open casket to show the world the brutality of the killing. "The open-coffin funeral held by Mamie Till Bradley exposed the world to more than her son Emmett till's bloated, mutilated body. Her decision focused attention not only on American racism and the barbarism of lynching but also on the limitations and vulnerabilities of American democracy." Tens of thousands attended his funeral or viewed his casket, and images of his mutilated body were published in black-oriented magazines and newspapers, rallying popular black support and white sympathy across the US. Intense scrutiny was brought to bear on the condition of black civil rights in Mississippi with newspapers around the country critical of the state. Although initially local newspapers and law enforcement officials decried the violence against Till and called for justice, they soon began responding to national criticism by defending Mississippians, which eventually transformed into support for the killers.

In September 1955, Bryant and Milam were acquitted of Till's kidnapping and murder. Protected against double jeopardy, Bryant and Milam publicly admitted in an interview with Look magazine that they killed Till. Problems identifying Till affected the trial, partially leading to Bryant's and Milam's acquittals, and the case was officially reopened by the United States Department of Justice in 2004. As part of the investigation, the body was exhumed and autopsied, resulting in a positive identification. He was reburied in a new casket, which is the standard practice in cases of body exhumation. His original casket was donated to the Smithsonian Institution.

Then there was the case of Rodney King! Rodney Glen King, III was an African-American taxi driver who became nationally known after being beaten by Los Angeles Police Department officers following a high-speed car chase on March 3, 1991. A witness, George Holliday, videotaped much of the beating from his balcony and sent the footage to local news station, KTLA. The footage shows four officers surrounding King, several of them striking him repeatedly, and while other officers stood by. Parts of the footage were aired around the world and raised public concern about police treatment of minorities in the United States.

Four officers were charged with assault with a deadly weapon and use of excessive force. Three were acquitted of all charges. The jury acquitted the fourth of assault with a deadly weapon but failed to reach a verdict on the use of excessive force. The jury deadlocked at 8 to 4 in favor of acquittal at the state level. The acquittals are generally considered to have triggered the 1992 Los Angeles riots in which 55 people were killed, and over 2,000 were injured, ending only when the California national guard was called in.

The acquittals also led to the federal government obtaining grand jury indictments for violations of King's civil rights. The trial of the four in a federal district court ended on April 16, 1993, with two of the officers being found guilty and subsequently imprisoned. The other two were acquitted again.

If that's not enough, then came the case of Trayvon Martin. On the night of February 26, 2012, in Sanford, Florida, George Zimmerman fatally shot Trayvon Martin, a 17-year-old African-American high school student. Zimmerman, a 28-year-old mixed race Hispanic man was the neighborhood watch coordinator for the gated community where Martin was temporarily living and where the shooting took place.

Zimmerman shot Martin, who was unarmed, during an altercation between the two. Responding to an earlier call from Zimmerman, police arrived on the scene within 2 minutes of the shooting. Zimmerman was taken into custody, treated for head injuries, then questioned for 5 hours. The police chief said that Zimmerman was released because there was no evidence to refute Zimmerman's claim of having acted in self-defense, and under Florida's Stand Your Ground statute, the police were prohibited by law from making an arrest. The police chief also said that Zimmerman had a right to defend himself with lethal force. As news of the case spread, thousands of protesters across the country called for Zimmerman's arrest and a full investigation. Six weeks after the shooting, amid widespread, intense, and in some cases, misleading media coverage. Zimmerman was charged with murder by a special prosecutor appointed by Governor Rick Scott. Zimmerman's trial began on June 10, 2013, in Sanford. On July 13, 2013, a jury acquitted him. On 24 February 2015, the United States Department of Justice announced that "there was not enough evidence for a federal hate crime prosecution."

I honestly feel that a neighborhood cop has no right to harass a minor. After he made the call to 911 and was instructed to stay in his car, all this would've never happened. He said he looked suspicious because he had on a black hoody, and houses were being broken into. So, he assumed and harassed a kid and murdered him. See, when you have a gun, you feel powerful. Any man can tell you that. You want to use it so bad, so I'm guessing because George Zimmerman never can pass his test to become a police officer, he did the next best thing he can do: become a neighborhood watch member so he can be powerful and have his gun on a teen and murder Trayvon Martin.

I had the pleasure of meeting Trayvon Martin's father Tracy Martin. He came into my store at the Pembroke Lakes Mall, and I gave him my condolences as he held his youngest daughter. I saw the pain in his eyes as you could see how much he loved to be a father to his children. I told him back then that I want to help young black males avoid racist cops and make a difference while here on earth. He gave me a Trayvon Martin bracelet right off his wrist, and I wore that bracelet every day to work. I would look at it every day and think to myself, I just want to live one more day to make a difference. The day that bracelet popped, I was angry, but Prince Motivation was already in effect. So, if Tracy Martin is reading this, I need another bracelet, my brother.

Next up, Mike Brown! The shooting of Michael Brown occurred on August 9, 2014, in Ferguson, Missouri, a northern suburb of St. Louis. Brown, an 18-year-old black man, was fatally shot by Darren Wilson, a 28-year-old, white, Ferguson police officer. The disputed circumstances of the shooting sparked existing tensions in the predominantly black city where protests and civil unrest erupted. The events received considerable attention in the US and elsewhere, attracting protesters from outside the region. They generated a vigorous national debate about the relationship between law enforcement and African-Americans, and about the police use-of-force doctrine in Missouri and nationwide. A St. Louis County grand jury decided not to indict Wilson, and he was exonerated of criminal wrongdoing by the United States Department of Justice.

Shortly before the shooting, Brown stole several packages of cigarillos from a nearby convenience store and shoved the store clerk who tried to stop him, per the U.S. Department of Justice examination. Brown was accompanied by his friend, Dorian Johnson. Wilson had been notified by police dispatch of the robbery and descriptions of the two suspects. He encountered Brown and Johnson as they were walking down the middle of the street. Wilson said that he realized that the two men matched the robbery suspects' descriptions. Wilson backed up his cruiser and blocked them. An altercation ensued with Brown and Wilson struggling through the window of the police vehicle for control of Wilson's gun until it was fired. Brown and Johnson then fled with Wilson in pursuit of Brown. Brown stopped and turned to face the officer, then Brown moved toward him. Wilson fired at Brown several times, all shots striking him in the front, except for the two bullets fired into Brown's right arm. In the entire altercation, Wilson fired a total of 12 bullets!!!!!; the last was probably the fatal shot. Brown was unarmed and moving toward Wilson when the final shots were fired. Witness reports differed as to what Brown was doing with his hands when he was shot, but the U.S. Department of Justice found that those witnesses who said that Brown had his hands up in surrender were not credible.

The shooting sparked unrest in Ferguson. The "hands up" account was widely circulated within the black community immediately after the shooting, and it contributed to the strong protests and outrage about the killing of the unarmed man. The U.S. Department of Justice did not conclude that the "hands up" account was inaccurate until months later. Believing accounts that Brown had his hands up in surrender when he was shot, protesters chanted, "Hands up, don't shoot." Protests, both peaceful and violent along with vandalism and looting continued for more than a week in Ferguson; police established a nightly curfew. The response of area police agencies in dealing with the protests was strongly criticized by the media and politicians. There were concerns over insensitivity, tactics, and a militarized response. Missouri Governor Jay Nixon ordered local police organizations to cede much of their authority to the Missouri State Highway Patrol.

A grand jury was called and given extensive evidence from Robert McCulloch, the St. Louis County Prosecutor. On November 24, 2014, McCulloch announced that the St. Louis County grand jury had decided not to indict Wilson. On March 4, 2015, the U.S. Department of Justice reported the conclusion of its own investigation and cleared Wilson of civil rights violations in the shooting. It found that forensic evidence supported the officer's account, witnesses who corroborated the officer's account were credible, and the witnesses who had incriminated him were not credible with some admitting that they had not directly seen the events. The U.S. Department of Justice concluded that Wilson shot Brown in self-defense. So, in other words, what they do is not credible, and what they say is credible. I believe in Karma, and these officers who are doing these hateful crimes must face their Karma.

My question is Where are the Taser guns? Why is it that every time police face young African-American men, the first thing they do is pull out their real guns and start killing our fathers? I believe these cops have clean records, and they never were ever faced with confrontations with African-Americans, and now, so many police officers are getting off. They are killing us and getting no convictions. Here are a couple more names: Sandra Bland, Kathryn Johnston, Sean Bell, Eric Garner, Rekia Boyd, Amadou Diallo, Kimani Gray, Kenneth Chamberlain, Travares McGill, Tamir Rice, Aiyana Stanley-Jones, Freddie Gray, and finally, Martin Luther King, Jr. How many people must die, and there is no resolution? I have been on record stating that I know that we need police, and there are some good ones. The bad ones to me are not cops or officers who protect and serve. We not being killed by police officers; we are being killed by the KKK members and their supporters, hiding behind the badges.

KKK, The Ku Klux Klan (KKK), or simply "the Klan," is the name of three distinct past and present movements in the United States that have advocated extremist reactionary currents, such as white supremacy, white nationalism, anti-immigration, and, especially in later iterations,

Nordics, anti-Catholicism, and antisemitism, historically expressed through terrorism aimed at groups or individuals whom they opposed. All three movements have called for the "purification" of American society, and all are considered right-wing extremist organizations. This hate group killed our great grandparents and leaders because of the color of their skin. My question is Where are they now? I'll tell you where they are. They are the people who throw their money on the counter when you put out your hand. The people that clutch their purses when they see you walk by. They are the judges in the court house who make decisions based on your past instead of your present. They are the cops who pull you over for no reason and harass you to provoke you. They are there in hiding, and we must protect ourselves and future leaders the youth.

When people say this, or hear #BlackLivesMatter, it doesn't mean it's the only ethnicity group that matters! It's just putting the world on notice that we matter too! R.I.P to all lives that were lost! People like Colin Kaepernick made a huge impact while I was in the process of writing this book. He took a knee during the National Anthem. Colin Kaepernick said, and I quote, "I am not going to stand up to show pride in a flag for a country that oppresses black people and people of color," Kaepernick told the NFL media in an exclusive interview after the game. "To me, this is bigger than football, and it would be selfish on my part to look the other way. There are bodies in the street and people getting paid leave and getting away with murder." I commend Colin Kaepernick for what he did. He started a trend and brought awareness to this issue, and I respect him for that. He used his platform the way he wanted to. People try to say he was against the military, and he was not. He is a man who was raised by white Americans and just had a problem with the way the world has been.

So, my take on police brutality is this. Stay away from police. If they pull you over, relax. Do not engage in small talk; they will try to trick you and provoke you. Let them write every ticket, and take those tickets to the Ticket Clinic. For nearly 30 years, the Ticket Clinic has been providing legal services to motorists charged with traffic offenses like speeding, suspended licenses, and DUI. Since 1987, their lawyers have defended over three million cases, and their national footprint includes 25 offices in Florida. Their goal is the following: Case Dismissed. No points, no school. Their legal team services the entire state of Florida, including Dade, Broward, Palm Beach, St. Lucie, Orange, Hillsborough, Lee, Osceola, and Volusia counties. They have developed procedures, a knowledge base of technicalities, and defense strategies over nearly 3 decades of representing clients in traffic court. The Ticket Clinic offers these services to drivers who believe in their rights to a fair trial is at stake with their driving record.

I do not believe you should call them sir, ma'am, unless they call you sir or ma'am. Show respect first and just get to your job or home or to your family. I'm going to say this: pull your pants up nationwide. When I use to walk around with a gun, I couldn't sag my pants because my pistol would fall on the floor. Stay out of the way of the police. A white man told me that becoming a police officer was the closest thing to God. He told me, they can pull you over, take you to jail, or take your life. My eyes lit up because I respected his feelings and aspirations to be in law enforcement, but protecting and serving his community never came out of his mouth. So please don't cut up or get ratchet when you come across police officers. Conduct yourself as a king and queen. You don't have to kiss their butts, but show them respect and they will leave you alone. Don't let them provoke you. A wise man once said, I lost the fight but won the war. The fight is the encounter, winning the war is staying alive . . .

CHAPTER 9 MY INFLUENCES

As I start this Chapter, I will be watching the last debate between Hillary Clinton and Donald Trump for the presidential campaign 2016. My influences to start Prince Motivation and my movement came from a lot of different places. My first reason for trying to do more in life than just sell shoes is because of my biggest support, biggest influence: my mother. My mother was the first lady to give me a chance to listen to music at a young age and love it. I fell in love with hip hop and dance moves of Michael Jackson. Michael Jackson clearly is the most iconic artist in the world ever. Michael Joseph Jackson was an American singer, songwriter, record producer, dancer, actor and philanthropist. Called the "King of Pop," his contributions to music, dance, and fashion along with his publicized personal life made him a global figure in popular culture for over 4 decades.

Listening to R&B and people like Bobby Brown at a young age always made me want to dance and have fun. Robert Barisford "Bobby" Brown is an American R&B singer, songwriter, dancer, and actor. Brown started his career as one of the front men of the R&B and pop group, New Edition, from its inception in 1978 until his forced exit from the group in 1985, following a period of misbehavior and rebellious behavior on his part. Starting a solo career, he became a success with his second album in 1988, Don't Be Cruel, which spawned several hit singles, including the self-penned, "My Prerogative," which became his signature hit. Brown had a string of top-ten hits on various Billboard charts between 1986 and 1993. Brown is noted as a pioneer of new jack swing, a fusion of R&B. Even to this day, when I get turned all the way up, I start to dance like a young Bobby Brown.

While growing up as an 80's baby, another huge artist was the great Tupac Shakur. Tupac Amaru Shakur, also known by his stage names, 2Pac and Makaveli, was an American rapper, record producer, and actor. As of 2007, Shakur had sold over 75 million records worldwide. His double disc albums, All Eyez on Me and his Greatest Hits, are among the best-selling albums in the United States. He has been listed and ranked as one of the greatest artists of all time by many magazines, including Rolling Stone, which ranked him 86th on its list of the 100 Greatest Artists of All Time. He is consistently ranked as one of the greatest rappers ever as well as one of the most influential rappers of all time. My mother loved him. I remember when my grandfather past away, she bought a nice gold flat chain like the one 2pac had. 2pac is still to this day the best rapper ever!

Growing up in Texas, I became a sports fan of the Dallas Cowboys. I attempted to play sports, but I was given that God-given gift to out run or out lift my friends and classmates. Jerral Wayne "Jerry" Jones, Sr. is an American businessman. On February 25, 1989, Jones purchased the Cowboys from H. R. "Bum" Bright for $140 million. Soon after the purchase, he fired longtime coach, Tom Landry, and to that point, the only coach in the team's history, in favor of his old teammate at Arkansas, Jimmy Johnson. He is the owner, president, and general manager of the NFL's Dallas Cowboys. Jones was born in Los Angeles, California. His family moved to North Little Rock, Arkansas, and Jones was a running back at North Little Rock High School. He attended college at the University of Arkansas where he was a member of the Kappa Sigma fraternity. He was also a co-captain of the 1964 National Championship football team. He was an All-Southwest Conference offensive lineman for Hall of Fame coach Frank Broyles and a teammate of Jimmy Johnson. Jones is one of a very small number of NFL owners who had a significant level of success as a football player.

The Dallas Cowboys now is the biggest sports franchise in all sports with a net worth of $4 billion dollars. One huge reason why was because of the hire of Jimmy Johnson and the huge Hershel Walker trade! Jimmy Johnson, James William Johnson, is an American football broadcaster and former player, coach, and executive. He served as the head football coach at Oklahoma State University–Stillwater from 1979 to 1983 and the University of Miami from 1984 to 1988. Johnson then moved to the National Football League, serving as head coach of the Dallas Cowboys from 1989 to 1993, winning two Super Bowls with the team, both against the Buffalo Bills, and the Miami Dolphins from 1996 to 1999. As of 2015, he is an analyst for Fox NFL Sunday, the Fox network's NFL pregame show for the NFL games. Jimmy Johnson was an influence on me because he always represented with style and grace. He was aggressive and wasn't scared to let his players know that they were either good, bad, or great. I found myself always keeping a fresh haircut like Jimmy, having fun with my staff like Jimmy, and I enjoyed winning like Jimmy. Only if Jimmy Johnson and Jerry Jones would have gotten along a little while longer. I don't ever see the Dallas Cowboys going down that losing spiral season after season, especially with the eye for talent that Jimmy Johnson has. I got that from Jimmy, too.

One of my favorite football players of all time is Randy Moss! Randy Gene Moss is a former American football wide receiver who played 14 seasons in the National Football League. He holds the NFL single-season touchdown reception record, the NFL single-season touchdown reception record for a rookie, and is second on the NFL all-time regular season touchdown reception list with 156. He is widely considered among the greatest wide receivers of all time. But the guy that has a big influence on my life is another guy who wore purple. I mentioned him earlier, Ray Lewis, when I mention my leader in George Jenkins. Raymond Anthony Lewis, Jr. is a former American football linebacker who played his entire 17-year career for the Baltimore Ravens of the National Football League. He played college football for the University of Miami, and earned All-America honors. Drafted by the Ravens in the first round in 1996, Lewis was the last active player from the team's inaugural season. Ray Lewis is probably one of the most inspiring, motivating, living legends to ever play middle linebacker in the NFL to me. The Ray Lewis story is about not having his father in his life, a point where he and I relate. Watching a strong, single mom like my mom raise him, I love how he used his pain to drive him to be great. I read in his book about how he did pushups to build up his body, and I did the same exact thing. I don't even bet my friends money anymore; I bet push-ups. Ray Lewis is a father to his children, and in interviews, he said he would break the curse his family had. Just like his father telling him, he wasn't in Ray's life because his dad wasn't in his life. My father told me the same thing. He didn't have a father in is life. That was an excuse because my father was married and chose not to be a part of my life. He was married and chose not to be there. It is what it is; he gave me life, and I'm forever grateful, but I will never forget all the hard times when I had no one to call dad. I, too, wanted to be a father, but I never had kids to bring into this world and break the mold, also. I wanted to meet Ray Lewis one day and maybe have him sign his book or just chill with him for one day. He has so much passion and knowledge. One day, I want to be great like him. He will be a first-ballot hall of famer.

I remember my very first day of school at Boyd Anderson, which is where I met my next influence. Coach Johnathan E. Williams was one of my teachers at the time of my freshman year. It started with the roll call. He went down the list, and I always know my name will come up when the teacher looks at my last name and becomes hesitant. So, he attempted to say it, and I helped him pronounce it (Mom like mom, premier like movie), and I believe he said, "Ok, that's a Haitian last name." I said, "No, it's French." I remember at the time one of my classmates, Magdala, looked back at me as I said, No, it's French!" knowing dang on well I was lying. I didn't embrace my heritage. But Coach Williams throughout that year help me build confidence and always taught me to accept who I am and never try to be anyone different. Coach Williams and Coach Otis Rollie, III talked me into trying out for the wrestling team. I went out and participated but got suspended one time for biting a kid. I had a Mike Tyson moment because the kid from Cardinal Gibbons covered my nose and mouth, and I couldn't breathe. So, I bit him and got suspended and that was my last year wrestling.

Coach Williams was a positive, great young teacher who went on to become the athletic director by my senior year, and most recently, he became the principal of Northeast High School. We stayed in touch through Facebook over the years, and I got a chance to see a side of Coach Williams I didn't get to see. He is a graduate from Florida State University with a degree in Political Science. He has been married for years to his wife Stacy Williams. He has three beautiful children and has been an active parent. He also keeps in touch with all his students. It's almost like everything fell into place. I one day want to go back to school and get some type of degree under my belt. I one day want to get married to a beautiful, strong, educated woman, have children, and always be there for people I interact with. Coach Williams, if you didn't know, now you know. You left a good impression on my life, and you are a reason I want to help the youth in a positive way.

There were a lot of coaches I liked, but with these next two guys, I'm going to talk about ways of coaching and leading I used to help me in my work environment. The first is Herm Edwards! Herman "Herm" Edwards, Jr. is an American football analyst and former National Football League player and coach. Since 2009, he has been a pro football analyst for ESPN. He played cornerback for 10 seasons with the Philadelphia Eagles, Los Angeles Rams, and Atlanta Falcons. Prior to his coaching career, Edwards was known best as the player who recovered a fumble by Giants quarterback, Joe Pisarcik, on a play dubbed the "Miracle at the Meadowlands." It was his rant that won me over on October 30, 2002! After a heartbreaking 24 to 21, Week 8 loss to the Cleveland Browns at the Meadowlands, head coach Herman Edwards gave his famous "You play to win the game" tirade in the post-game press conference. I laughed, but he was telling the truth. He is also a motivational speaker, and I see some of his speeches given to young athletes all over the nation. He is professional, sharp, and real. I want to be motiving like him because every day, I clock in to work. The quota I'm going against is my opponent. The other sneaker stores in my mall is like the other teams in the same division, and I plan to be better than them and win the game every day, and every week.

The second is Bill Belichick! I know I'm a Cowboy fan, but this guy is special. William Stephen "Bill" Belichick is an American football coach who is the head coach of the New England Patriots of the National Football League. Belichick has extensive authority over the Patriots' football operations, effectively making him the general manager of the team as well. He was previously the head coach of the Cleveland Browns. Belichick began his coaching career in 1975, and by 1985, he was the Defensive Coordinator for New York Giants head coach, Bill Parcells. Parcells and Belichick won two Super Bowls together (XXI and XXV) before Belichick left to become the head coach in Cleveland in 1991. He remained in Cleveland for five seasons and was fired following the team's 1995 season. Belichick then rejoined Parcells, first in New England and later with the New York Jets. After being named head coach of the Jets in early 2000, Belichick resigned after only one day on the job to accept the head coaching job for the New England Patriots. Since then, he has coached the Patriots to six Super Bowl appearances. His teams won Super Bowls XXXVI, XXXVIII, XXXIX, and XLIX and lost Super Bowls XLII and XLVI. He has led the Patriots to 13 AFC East division titles and 10 appearances in the AFC Championship Game. He was named the AP NFL Coach of the Year for the 2003, 2007, and 2010 seasons.

Belichick is the NFL's longest-tenured active head coach and currently is fourth in regular season coaching wins in the NFL at 232 and first in playoff coaching wins with 23. He completed his 40th season as an NFL coach in 2014 and won his fourth Super Bowl, tying Pittsburgh's Chuck Noll for the most Super Bowl wins by a head coach. He is one of only five head coaches with four or more titles in NFL history. He is also the only head coach in NFL history to win three Super Bowl championships in a four-year span. They fired him, and that didn't break him. He got his second opportunity after losing his job and has become a household name. The thing I love when people talk about him is the Patriot Way. He is not flashy and sometimes to other people, he is a bit boring. I think the job he did against the Buffalo Bills as a defensive coordinator with the New York Giants was great. Bill Belichick shocked the world by stopping the high-scoring Buffalo Bills. His interviews are hilarious because he sticks to the subjects and ignores anyone who tries to trick him out of his position. Like Bill at work, I don't really smile that much. I hire people around me that are very bubbly and smile a lot. I like my team to be friendly because customers lie and try to get over. Like Bill Belichick preaches to his team, DO YOUR JOB! That's all I want. I have never seen the reason to kiss ass and not get the job done. I believe if you work for someone and getting paid, you should give 110% unless you are not feeling well or injured to the point you can't physically do your job. In my stores, I created the mindset: no days off! You get days off, but you should always grind!

I say grind because of Eric Thomas. Eric D. Thomas is an American motivational speaker, author, and minister. Speeches by Thomas have been widely viewed and are popular on YouTube. Thomas was born in Chicago, Illinois, and grew up in Detroit, Michigan. After an argument with his parents, he dropped out of high school and was homeless on the streets of Detroit for 2 years. I was homeless like him with no one to help. He went back to school and got his degree late, just like I'm in pursuit of. This year, I decided to go back to school and get a degree, also. I saw his famous video on YouTube: you must want to succeed as bad as you want to breathe. Pushed me to work harder than anyone. I want to be like Eric and travel the world once I start speaking and motivating people as well. He is a very nice brother; I had the pleasure of meeting him as I attended one of his seminars. A very memorable experience.

Magdala (Maggie) and I eventually became close while attending BA. She told me that she had a brother who was going to transfer into school. Her brother was Jimmy Desinord. Jimmy and I became close. We stayed very close to each other in Lauderhill. We would hang out and grow a unique friendship over the years. Jimmy and would share family stories or situations and grow a brotherhood that now is unbreakable. Jimmy was from the Bahamas but spoke better creole than me. Jimmy was the quiet type, and I was the loud always-wanted-to-be-seen type of guy. I was into sports, and Jimmy was into sport cars. I like the ratchet of all ratchet hood girls, and Jimmy was into the quiet girls who were from all ethnicities. Jimmy never turned his back on me, and always looked out for me when I didn't have. He never laughed at me when I was down. Jimmy even took me to my first strip club, and yall are thinking he was quiet, lol. Jimmy has a little bit of hood in him. We would go to the hood club, and Jimmy would go only because he knew that's where I wanted to go and have fun. He always was a team player.

If I had a dollar for every time people tell us yall are complete opposites, I probably wouldn't have to write and sell this book. But one thing about Jimmy is he is a loyal, hardworking man, and everyone I introduce him to, they love him. He is short like too short, but he has a heart bigger than anyone I know. My family loves him, and I love him. We already know whenever one of us gets married, we are going to be each other's best man. Jimmy Desinord means a lot to me; he is my brother. The first child Jimmy had was Jayden Desinord and guess who he names the Godfather? ME (Kolyon voice)! Jimmy is a positive brother to me. He taught me how to be a professional even though he and I work in two different fields. He taught me how to manage people and be a leader. I'm forever grateful I met Jimmy; he is a brother from another mother. I have his back forever.

Throughout my life, movies had a big impact and influence in my life as well. Movies like the classic, Lean on Me, had a big influence on me. Lean on Me is a 1989 dramatized biographical film written by Michael Schiffer, directed by John G. Avildsen, and starring Morgan Freeman. Lean on Me is loosely based on the story of Joe Louis Clark, a real inner city high school principal in Paterson, New Jersey, whose school was at risk of being taken over by the New Jersey state government unless the students improved their test scores on the New Jersey Minimum Basic Skills Test. The character, Mr. Clark, as the new principal, was relatable to me as a young upcoming retail manager. It's pretty much a must for every manager in my field to be responsible to make to come in a create change if you want to succeed and become successful. It's hard making young kids buy into what you want to build or achieve. I wasn't always this positive motivational prince you are reading about. When I was young, I felt that everybody should want to attack customers and love making money. Some people I met along the way got away with murder and didn't have to work hard to get hours or a promotion. I never respected that because I had to work hard for everything I ever had. I couldn't stomach spoiled kids. But I learned that everyone isn't like me or was brought up like me. The life lessons Mr. Clarke instilled in those kids and the way they embraced him by the end of the film makes it one of my all-time favorites. I'm very strict and stern just like Mr. Clarke was in that movie played by Morgan Freeman.

Another film is the movie, Rudy. Rudy has always been told that he was too small to play college football. But he was determined to overcome the odds and fulfill his dream of playing for Notre Dame. One of the best scenes that I relate to the most was when Rudy was about to quit football. The custodian looked at him and gave him a great speech and just told him all the things he overcame. All the positive things that happened for him in route to trying to dress to play on the field with the Fighting Irish. I had a moment in my life when that happened to me. I felt like giving up and quitting at times. It was at my first store as a manager. I would work open to close, back to back to back, and wouldn't get any help. My friend, Corey Johns, talked me into to staying with the company.

Corey was a veteran who been with the company for years and for whom also I found as a great friend. He was a young store manager as well and went through similar problems that I was going through. He treated me like a brother from day one because I drove up the road to meet him and help him. We have been cool ever since. Corey was older than me and taught me a lot about not giving up because I was good at what we do. He showed me that you can have fun with your team to an extent. I was always against it. We were inseparable, and we acted like brothers. Spent holidays together, and like Jimmy, with his next child, Corey named me his daughter, Alatza Johns', godfather. Corey is engaged and has a beautiful family. He has a beautiful fiancé my close friend Amber. They have five beautiful daughters in total and three pit bulls. Corey is a big influence in my life because he has always put family first and treats me like family. I wouldn't be where I'm at right now with the ranking I have or even with the company that I work for if it wasn't for Corey. I'm forever grateful to have met Corey too.

One of my other closets friends that's an influence on me is my big brother James Fernando Monde. I'm sure when he first met me, he probably thought I was this conceited manager who thought he was all that. I just transfer into a new district and received a store that many people wanted. They don't know I turned down that offer two times previously. The reason why I finally said yes was because I pretty much got fed up of the jealously and malicious treatment I received while at my former store. So of course, I know the drill, it's like being the new employee with a title and others want to see if you deserved it or waiting for you to fail. James was someone I had small conversations with until we found out we had a lot in common. We both like sports he just has bad taste in teams. He like the rival New York Giants of my Dallas Cowboys. He likes the

New York Knicks and I like the Los Angeles Lakers. He is from up North New York and I'm from the South Texas and Florida.

So, we are different but have the same morals and principles and that's where we relate a lot and grew a friendship. It has been tested with any brotherhood or friendship will. Where you find out if you will fall out or your friend is always honest. James is very thorough and real. His heart is bigger than anyone I know. He is a great father and loves helping people. He is Haitian like myself and works hard for everything it's in our blood. We both work in the same field and have a great friend in Anson who he brought me and him closer. It was a time where he had me and Anson have a sit down because of some male chatty patty and me n Anson been tight ever since as well. James finds positive out of any situation. He is a lot different from most of my childhood friends because he is a little bit older and he can peep certain characteristics about people I may slip on. He always gives me good advice about relationships or anything I have on my mind. We workout out together sometimes and just talk about life. The stories we share when we go to Vista View Park are kept between us and are very important. You got to have that one friend that isn't scared to tell you "You messed up r I don't agree with you". Any friend I bring him around they all say he is good peoples. I learn a lot through James and he makes me better. One day me and my mom was in the mall getting her eyes check. I look up and she smiled so hard because she seen James rocking my Prince Motivation shirt with her dad's name across the top. I will never forget that moment in my life. You should have friends like this if you want to be a lot more positive in life. I thank God for the relationship me and my brother James have, he is honestly a brother from a different mother.

I appreciate hard work and greatness so for me Floyd Mayweather Jr. is the epidemy of that. Floyd Joy Mayweather Jr. is an American former professional boxer who competed from 1996 to 2015, and currently works as a boxing promoter. Widely considered to be one of the greatest boxers of all time, undefeated as a professional, and a five-division world champion, Mayweather won fifteen world titles and the lineal championship in four different weight classes. He is a two-time winner of The Ring Magazine's Fighter of the Year award, a three-time winner of the Boxing Writers Association of America Fighter of the Year award, and a six-time winner of the Best Fighter ESPY Award. In 2016 Mayweather peaked as Boxer's number one pound for pound fighter of all time; as well as the greatest welterweight of all time. In 2016, ESPN ranked Mayweather as the greatest pound for pound boxer of the last 25 years.

Floyd Mayweather went 49-0 in his career, which is one win short of beating Rocky Marciano's record! He left the sport of boxing on his terms. He invested his money back into himself into

TMT acronym for the money team. He is very wealthy and very his smart. Everyone he faced he beat. He has been criticizing but never has been beaten. See I learned over time, people will say things all day long to throw you off your game. Try to trick you out your position because you have talents and attributes of someone great. Every day you wake up you have the option to be bad, okay, good, or great. It starts with you. Floyd didn't go to the gym and cry about what his father did when he helps other fighters against him. He went to his gym and worked. Some people don't like a young black successful African American man with money. It's the life unfortunately we live in, but Floyd Mayweather has inspired me to get up every day and get to work.

There is another boxer that passed away that has inspired me and millions worldwide Muhammad Ali! Muhammad Ali was an American professional boxer and activist. He was widely regarded as one of the most significant and celebrated sports figures of the 20th century. From early in his career, Ali was known as an inspiring, controversial, and polarizing figure both inside and outside the ring. I never witness him fight via television or live. But I watch his movie played by a man I greatly respect in Will smith. I was moved, and it made me go and watch his interviews. Watch his press conference before fights. I watch the way he had confidence and fear no man. I see the way he was a father to his children, and husband to his wife. Cassius Clay was born and raised in Louisville, Kentucky, and began training as an amateur boxer when he was 12 years old. At age 18, he won a gold medal in the light heavyweight division at the 1960 Summer Olympics in Rome, after which he turned professional later that year. At age 22 in 1964, he won the WBA, WBC and lineal heavyweight titles from Sonny Liston in an upset. Clay then converted to Islam and changed his name from Cassius Clay, which he called his "slave name", to Muhammad Ali. He set an example of racial pride for African Americans and resistance to white domination during the 1960s Civil Rights Movement.

In 1966, two years after winning the heavyweight title, Ali further antagonized the white establishment in the U.S. by refusing to be conscripted into the U.S. military, citing his religious beliefs and opposition to American involvement in the Vietnam War. He was eventually arrested, found guilty of draft evasion charges and stripped of his boxing titles. He successfully appealed in the U.S. Supreme Court, which overturned his conviction in 1971, by which time he had not fought for nearly four years—losing a period of peak performance as an athlete. Ali's actions as a conscientious objector to the war made him an icon for the larger counterculture generation.

Ali is regarded as one of the leading heavyweight boxers of the 20th century. He remains the only three-time lineal heavyweight champion, having won the title in 1964, 1974 and 1978.

Between February 25, 1964, and September 19, 1964, Ali reigned as the undisputed heavyweight champion. He is the only boxer to be named The Ring Magazine Fighter of the Year six times. He was ranked as the greatest athlete of the 20th century by Sports Illustrated and the Sports Personality of the Century by the BBC. ESPN Sports Century ranked him the third greatest athlete of the 20th century. Nicknamed "The Greatest", he was involved in several historic boxing matches. Notable among these were the first Liston fight; the "Fight of the Century", "Super Fight II" and the "Thrill in Manila" versus his rival Joe Frazier; and "The Rumble in the Jungle" versus George Foreman.

At a time when most fighters let their managers do the talking, Ali thrived in—and indeed craved—the spotlight, where he was often provocative and outlandish. He was known for trash talking, and often freestyled with rhyme schemes and spoken word poetry, both for his trash talking in boxing and as political poetry for his activism, anticipating elements of rap and hip hop music. As a musician, Ali recorded two spoken word albums and a rhythm and blues song, and received two Grammy Award nominations. As an actor, he performed in several films and a Broadway musical. Ali wrote two autobiographies, one during and one after his boxing career.

As a Muslim, Ali was initially affiliated with Elijah Muhammad's Nation of Islam (NOI) and advocated their black separatist ideology. He later disavowed the NOI, adhering initially to Sunni Islam and later to Sufism, and supporting racial integration, like his former mentor Malcolm X. After retiring from boxing in 1981, Ali devoted his life to religious and charitable work. In 1984, Ali was diagnosed with Parkinson's syndrome, which his doctors attributed to boxing-related brain injuries. As the condition worsened, Ali made limited public appearances and was cared for by his family until his death on June 3, 2016 in Scottsdale, Arizona. Watching the coverage of his funeral and seeing all the people in route to where he was buried was special. The car was covered with roses people threw on the limo that he body was riding in, and they stuck to the windshield.

I still haven't decided where but I want a Martin Luther King Jr. tattoo. Martin Luther King Jr. was an American Baptist minister and activist who was a leader in the African-American Civil Rights Movement. He is best known for his role in the advancement of civil rights using nonviolent civil disobedience based on his Christian beliefs. I have seen a lot of videos and read speeches of the great Dr. King. He is one of the biggest influences in my life. I always said I want to be great like Martin but I have an attitude like Malcom X. He is one man I would pay to go back in time to just have a one conversation with him. I know he grew up in church and always put God first. For someone like myself who believes in God but don't just limit myself to one religion. I would ask him how did he stay so positive and poise throughout all the hate. That's very tough what he went thru, but the outcome of his life and legacy is just a milestone any human being would want to have and leave.

My brother Malcom X is also a big influence in my life. Malcolm X, born Malcolm Little and later also known as el-Hajj Malik el-Shabazz, was an African-American Muslim minister and human rights activist. To his admirers, he was a courageous advocate for the rights of blacks, a man who indicted white America in the harshest terms for its crimes against black Americans; detractors accused him of preaching racism and violence. He has been called one of the greatest and most influential African Americans in history. I love his attitude, the passion and the voice he speaks with when he has always behind any pulpit. I watch his movie directed by Spike Lee and I believe is probably hands down the best life documentary of all time. I see a lot of Malcom X instill in me. When I put on my Ray Ban prescript glasses at an awards meeting and I took a picture at the hotel. I put it side by side by a Malcom X picture in the past and it's almost a spitting image of Malcom X. I have the courage to stand up to any leader or superior like he did. I want to get a big X tattoo on my body somewhere just to pay homage to him.

Another Muslim man brother I look up to, is Minister Louis Farrakhan. Louis Farrakhan, Sr. is an American religious leader, activist, and social commentator. He is the leader of the religious group Nation of Islam and served as the minister of major mosques in Boston and Harlem, and was appointed by the   longtime NOI leader, Elijah Muhammad, as the National Representative of the Nation of Islam. After Wraith Den Muhammad disbanded the NOI and started the orthodox Islamic group American Society of Muslims, Farrakhan started rebuilding the NOI. In 1981, he revived the name Nation of Islam for his organization, previously known as Final Call, regaining many of the Nation of Islam's National properties including the NOI National Headquarters Mosque Maryam, reopening over hundred thirty NOI mosques in America and the world. The Southern Poverty Law Center describes Farrakhan as anti-Semitic and a proponent of an anti-white theology. Farrakhan himself, however, disputes this view of his ideology.

I love my brother he always stands and speaks his truth. He humbles himself when he thinks he is wrong. He has read some many books he is so intelligent and he has inspired me to read more. I love watching most of his interviews from back in the days even his most recent on the famous Breakfast Club on 5/24/16. The think I love about him is he lets people know he is not a political man he is a religious man. He recognizes that he is a powerful leader and always make sure that words himself very well. I want the same respect and discipline he has when he speaks. I want to lead the next generation as he would. The rules that Farrakhan has taught me is to say to my enemy Peace be Upon them. He teaches to me to set up no God but one God, we should not steal, not commit murder, we should not bare false witness against thy neighbor, and we should not covet what belongs to someone else. He said long time ago, "Real joy is visioning something, and bringing it into life"! If I can ever just spend a day with him I would love to. I believe he is hated by so many people because he is powerful and he preaches what other races do not want us to know. Sort of how slave masters didn't want negroes to learn how to read or write so we can't be smart or know our truth. I'm so eager to learn more about the Muslim religion because of people like Farrakhan, Malcom X, Kevin Gates. These individuals are probably the biggest influence up to date in my life.

It was 2014 I wanted to buy a house because the cost of living in Florida is very expensive. I got the bad news that with my credit I couldn't borrow a penny from a bank. It was very embarrassing. I was making $62,000 a year with my company, but I didn't master the skill of saying "No". I was lending money to family and friends that never gave it back but I felt obligated. So, what do I do ask for my money back from people I know didn't have it. I was in a tough spot. I couldn't re-new my lease because I was already living in the red. I was in Debt. I was living outside my needs. I got advice from my older sister and she told me to think about down grading. It was crazy because my financial adviser at the bank told me the same thing. I had to eliminate my biggest expense which was rent! Where would I live if everywhere was too high? One key thing that I learn in this tough time in my life that I teach with my financial services "Is learning what your needs and wants are"! So, all I need was a room to lay my head, because all I do is work. So, finding a 1 bedroom was the best option.

I looked everywhere, I even thought about moving back to Lauderdale because rent is cheaper than in Pembroke Pines. I lucked up and met Sabne Noel my next influence I want to introduce to you. We were complete strangers, but she told me when she met me that if I was to live with her I had to love Family! Family? What does she mean family? I love my mom and my sister of course I love family. Little did I know she would change my definition of family. The day I met her, I also met her mom. They were also Haitian and told me that I would be treated as family from here on out. So, I had to put my pride to side and not have my own place anymore. That's tough. I couldn't walk around my crib naked anymore, I couldn't play my music loud while I cleaned up, and I had to trade in my bachelor pad for a small room that was like what a college student must stay in when they are earning they degrees. It would a setback for a major comeback. From the day, I moved in she became my second mother. The day Corey and my other homeboys help me move in she already told me I had to many sneakers. She had me sign a contract and all about buying shoes telling me that's how I was wasting my money. I'm looking at her like, she crazy but she was making sense.

A reason why Sabne Noel is so dear to my heart, is because she welcomed a stranger into her house with her family and children, and taught me life all over again. She wanted to guide me to success, and not end up like the rest. She has a sweet nice voice that has the power of understanding and communicates effectively. She uses the shoe example to tell me, I have all these shoes but no house. I had all this extra money and didn't invest into myself. Living with Sabne Noel daily was very interesting. She has given me relationship advise in and out of relationships. I have traveled with her and see what she means to her family out of the state of Florida. The way she loves her mother and has the patience to deal with her needs and her children needs is amazing. I watch this lady work 2 jobs over the age of 50 and makes no excuses. I watch her discipline herself to lose over 70 pounds in 6 months, so she can look stunning to see her daughter graduate from Case Western Reserve University. Sabne Noel has giving me tough love, and makes me do chores and I'm grown. She is the sole reason, and one of the people to just push me to go back to school. When I have a tough decision to make and she is off work at home. She makes time to listen to me, give me her side and point of view on the matter and gives me the best advice. She is a great mother to her two amazing kids my now brother and sister Joshua and Victoria Bouillon! She is a well-respected Nurse for more years than I lived! She has a work ethic that I don't believe Kevin Gates can keep up with. Her heart is amazing and I thank God, he brought her into my life. I honestly think me making the move, was a way for God to bring Sabne Noel to my life. She is the angel that has guided back on the right track, to go back and become who I'm destined to be. I love her just as much as I love Rosana Mompremier. She holds a special place in my heart, and I owe her a lot. Thank you Sabne for everything I will never forget all the little and big things you have done for me.

LiL Wayne Dwayne Michael Carter Jr., known professionally as Lil Wayne, is an American hip hop recording artist and author from New Orleans, Louisiana. In 1991, at the age of nine, Lil Wayne joined Cash Money Records as the youngest member of the label, and half of the duo The B.G.'z, alongside fellow New Orleans-based rapper Lil' Doogie. In 1996, Lil Wayne joined the southern hip hop group Hot Boys, with his Cash Money label-mates Juvenile, Young Turk and Lil' Doogie. Hot Boys debuted with Get It How U Live! that same year. Most of the group's success came with their platinum-selling album Guerrilla Warfare and the 1999 single "Bling Bling." Along with being the flagship artist of Cash Money Records, Lil Wayne is also the Chief Executive Officer of his own label imprint, Young Money Entertainment, which he founded in

2005. To me LiL Wayne has made countless motivational chart topping records. Best rapper Alive is a song a listen to on repeat when I'm running the hills for my cardio. I think LiL Wayne has the best-looking baby mommas in the world. Think about it Toya Carter, Sarah Vivan, actress Lauren London (New New), and Nivea! That song him and Nivea made "She Feeling Me" still jamming to me. I'm rocking with the Legend LiL Wayne because he is misunderstood at times. Let me say this the Reason LiL Wayne is considered Top 5 Rap artist ever is because he separates himself from the world. He doesn't watch the daily News he watches Sports Center and ESPN and if he is not doing that he is working on his craft or skateboarding. When you that great you eat and sleep rap. 2nd LiL Wayne wouldn't be here living or able be to do this interview because his life was saved by a white cop who rushed him to the hospital for shooting himself. So, I and I think everyone should respect his opinion because he may not know about police brutality or Black Lives Matter. T.I went hard on him thru social media, and has his right to use his platform how he wants. I just think that the same rules apply for Wayne. Let him use his platform as he wants. Obviously like he said he is rich and the white man is filming him. He hasn't had the experience you may have had. I have nothing against what he said. I close by saying this When we speak on current events, politics, or religion you must first respect someone's opinion because their life is not like yours or experience what you experience.

Speaking of T.I, he is also an influence on me. Clifford Joseph Harris Jr., better known by his stage names T.I. and Tip, is an American rapper and actor from Atlanta, Georgia. He signed his first major-label record deal in 1999, with Arista Records subsidiary, LaFace Records. In 2001, T.I. formed the Southern hip hop group Pimp Squad Click, alongside his longtime friends and fellow Atlanta-based rappers. Upon being released from Arista, T.I. signed to Atlantic Records and subsequently became the co-chief executive officer of his own label imprint, Grand Hustle Records, which he launched in 2003. T.I. is also perhaps best known as one of the artists who popularized the hip hop subgenre trap music, along with Young Jeezy and Gucci Mane. T.I business man, family man, actor, motivator, rapper, entertainer. A role model to me and someone I still would want to be like before I'm six feet under. I respect T. I's hustle! He created a clothing line hustle gang, and akoo. A.K.O.O. is a clothing line started in late 2008 and founded by T.I. and Jason Geter, both co-founders of Atlanta-based recording label Grand Hustle Records. A.K.O.O. is an acronym that stands for "A King of Oneself." Grand Hustle Records, also known as Hustle Gang Music, is an Atlanta, Georgia-based record label, founded in 2003, by American hip hop recording artist T.I. and his business partner Jason Geter. Up until December 2012, the label was distributed by Atlantic Records. It currently operates as an independent record label. The label is home to artists such as B.o.B, Young Dro, Trae tha Truth and Travis Scott, among others. The label also houses a roster of record producers, including DJ Toomp, Lil' C, Khao, Mars, Nard & B, TrackSlayerz and more. He is the true definition of a soldier that has overcome all adversity in life. He is talented in respected in my book for years. He is now stressing is concerns for all black people and I love that. I salute his efforts and work he has done.

Kevin Gates is my next influence I will want to spend some time to explain. Kevin Jerome Gilyard, better known by his stage name Kevin Gates, is an American rapper, singer, and entrepreneur from Baton Rouge, Louisiana. He is currently signed to Atlantic Records along with his own record label, Bread Winners' Association. His debut studio album, Islah, was released in January 2016 and peaked at number two on the US Billboard two hundred chart. I bought two copies, one for both of my cars! Prior to Islah, Gates also released numerous mixtapes including Stranger Than Fiction, By Any Means, and Luca Brasi two, all of which peaked in the top 40 on the Billboard two hundred chart. I must be honest I never heard of Kevin Gates until I heard some guy likes to eat booty. So, one day I said let me go watch this interview he did with DJ Whoo Kid. I understood what he meant. He just loves to please his woman. Who wouldn't? He is married to a beautiful woman and a great active father to his own and his kids that's not his. Its men walking around now that don't take care of their own kids. That speaks volumes to me because I grew up without a father like he did. He should be respected and looked out just on another light with that. So, then I watch his Breakfast Club Interview 8/27/15 and the way he started the interview impressed me. He said you gotta respect yourself and everything around you. I watch the whole interview I said let me go listen to his mixtape "By Any Means" I was impressed and I started to follow him.

It was around the time where I was not getting promoted to a position that I felt at the time I deserved. So now I was a big fan of Kevin Gates on my personal page before I created Prince Motivation I post his quotes some little videos on all my social media outlets. I learn so much important things thru his music. When I listen to Kevin Gates for the first time I said this guy is talented. I got to see him perform in 2014 in Pembroke Pines and people didn't know him. His music help me get promoted in 2015 real talk. When I listen to Kevin Gates I listen to the pain and the message. When I listen to these interviews, he says and jokes about things I would. It's not shade when he speaks; it's just comical truth in a way. I think that he is misunderstood. A lot of people can learn a lot from him if they don't judge just listen to him.

So, I was in a relationship with a young lady that was glued to social media, and always on it. It was plus for a little bit and beneficial when it came to this part of my book. Mind you I never met someone I became a fan of, but that was about to change. One day I was at work, and my ex-girlfriend mention my name under a picture post Kevin Gates made for some shoes he wanted. Out of thousands of people who were mention under that picture he responded to me. I don't know if he looked at my page and seen sneakers or me being a fan and having his pictures and quotes. So, we conversed backed in fourth and eventually I used my connections to help him out. He was in New York and I was in Florida and I got him what he wanted some Pro Modell Adidas in two colors. He sent a message through one of my friends in New York whenever he sees me he would look out. When he got off tour sure enough I seen his engineer and body guard come into my store. Right then and there I spoke to them and he Facetime Kevin Gates right there. Kevin Gates said thank you and invited me to a studio where he was going to be that night. I believed that's the same studio he recorded "The Truth". Man, I was excited to get off work, the hours couldn't move no slower that night. I called my ex and told her what happen of course she took all the credit, but I had to thank her.

So, that night I got off work and Kevin Gates greeted me with no security and just told me he appreciates everything I did for him. He told me he says people don't understand he still human and he appreciate still the small things. That night I watch his work ethic. I saw how respectful him and his brother Ron were with another artist. I saw how he created his music and sixteen bars and long it took him to make it right and put it all together. His energy and fun free spirit made everyone feel comfortable. He treated me like family and put me in the small, little video. One thing that impressed me about Kevin Gates after the track was laid and we took pictures. I saw Kevin Gates and his friends pray. That was powerful as I pulled off and left the studio in Miami I was on cloud nine. In that one night, I met my favorite artist, talk to him, took pictures, and learn a lot from him.

So, he gave me the encouragement to push this book and my Prince Motivation movement. I gave him a shirt and I'm dying to see him in it still. As I type this Kevin Gates has been sentenced to six months for a mistake he made. One thing about Kevin though he learns from his mistakes, and he taught me a lot of life lessons. Stand up what you believe in. I'm going to respect you and you supposed to do the same. If someone is beneficial to someone, why doesn't everything stop. Be with someone who you know you can't live without. Never let someone trick you out of your position. Every reaction doesn't need a reaction. He is another reason why I started to read Qur'an and learn more a lot of Allah and the Muslim religion. Hopefully we meet again and I can give Kevin Gates this book, because he has motivated me the most than any human being on earth. He has face so much adversity and he Is overcoming everything he is faced with. This is a minor setback for a major comeback. I want to thank Allah which means God for helping me cross paths with Kevin Gates and giving me the courage and ability to write this book. One thing I learned and will always remember is Kevin Gates told me. "People don't understand it's the smallest things in life, that matter the most" My small session and time with Kevin was the biggest impact and moment in my life!

While proof reading my final copy of this book. Kevin Gates served a five-month sentence for assaulting a fan, Gates was arrested upon his release on a weapons charge and had been in jail since late March. The "2 Phones" rapper finally found out what would happen to him on Wednesday when he was sentenced to 30 months in jail. So, if my dream comes true and Kevin is reading this is. I love you big brother, you a legend.

Music is a love and big influence I have and its apparent after you reached this part of the book. I just never was as talented as some of my friends or stars where I'm from and raised. I competed in talented shows at a young age, and did some freestyle battles at little, local clubs. I recorded in some hole in the wall studio's but never devoted time to rapping. So, when I hear my friend Reggie King A.K.A J.A.P. music and its motivating it makes me smile. I know he been through a lot, and I been his friend through it all. Supporting him when I can, and watching him grow as a man. Jap got acid thrown on him, he fell off a truck almost died with a skull fracture. He got in a terrible car accident, almost shot himself cleaning his gun. He got his wrist cut by accident with one of his cousin fighting over a knife. He broke both his legs and arms, and got hit by a truck in a hit and run. He, like myself, is protected by the highest. We both are very knowledgeable about Allah. He lost his mother at an early age. Watching him build his own brand SB (Soul Brothers), and getting better every year at rapping. He doesn't know it but he motivates me to build my own brand. Create something like Prince Motivation to encourage people from my city as he does. I really believe in him, and I know one day, he is going to make a lot of people proud! He has a great team around him and people like Yoshi the CEO of SME is keeping him focused. That's my brother for life, never did anything to me to question his loyalty. It's a lot of people from Broward I respect from a far in Broward County because it has its parts that are rough. They say if you can make it in New York, you can make it anywhere. I can say the exact same thing about Broward County. In cities where all you have is poverty strict environments where all you can look up to sometimes is drug dealers. That's exactly how I fell in love with Monte

Carlo SS. I always seen them on 4's that's 24 inch rims with a beautiful red bone in the passenger seat.

You have rap artists like Ridiculous Rowe who continues to grind and put his all in his music. Seeing the evolution of A.G Almighty who I went to school with at Boyd Anderson, and faced his adversity. Seeing him in different countries shooting videos, and seeing him in videos making appearances with the greats like Cam'ron, Rick Ross, and Gucci. Its saying something about people from Broward County! I said Kolyon voice earlier in my book, Kolyon is another upcoming rapper from Broward whom I never met but inspires me with his music. It was a song he dropped called Teamwork I heard off his mixtape Koly Luther King that made me realize how important my surroundings and staff at work meant to me. I listen to music before that, but he got hits and my other favorite rapper in LiL Boosie signed him.

Finally, is Kodak Black! Dieuson Octave, better known by his stage name Kodak Black, is an American hip hop recording artist. Octave was born on June 11, 1997 in Pompano Beach, Florida, where he was also raised. His parents were immigrants from Haiti. Octave was raised by his mother in Golden Acres, a public housing project in Pompano Beach. I'm not going to lie at first I was like I can't listen to these 90's babies they to wild. Then I had to look in the mirror and say I use to do dumb things too. I see a young man I'm very proud of. Being of Haitian decent is already at times challenging. Parents are very strict and love money. I saw when his mother cried as she seen her son in the double XXL covered. At that moment, I salute the Young King because he made is mother proud. I know my mother would react the same way. Hearing songs like Skrilla made me a fan. His mixtape LiL Big Pac to me is better than some major label artist albums. He has a gift and I understand him. While writing this book, he was release from jail, and the first video he recorded probably at his house got over 1 million views on YouTube in one week. I put out a list of my Top 5 artists from Broward County and mention these 5 young men, but the young Kodak has put the spot light on Broward County nationwide. From Drake dancing to his music on a private jet. Soulja Boy tried to ruin his career but failed. To seeing Free Kodak shirts nationwide it motivates me. Just recently Lamar Jackson an American football quarterback for the Louisville Cardinals. He won the Heisman Trophy, Maxwell Award, and Walter Camp Award and was a unanimous All-American as a sophomore in 2016. He is from Broward County as well and all he listens to is Kodak Black. I never saw a major artist from up north come down and shot a video with anyone from Broward. Kodak did him and French Montana calibrated on a track called Lock Jaw that went Gold. So clearly the five artists I mention are not the only successful and talented artist in Broward County. But for me, those 5 are in my opinion the best for now, and I know we have a lot more to come. I believe in Broward and will continue to hold my L up in photos and let people know I'm not ashamed of where I come from. I love my city will continue to root from Broward County and anyone who comes from Broward County. It challenges me want to be the best motivational speaker in the nation as well, and say yup he came from Broward County too.

CHAPTER 10 WHAT IS PRINCE MOTIVATION?

I heard the late great Al Davis say every great leader has some ruthless to them, and sometimes you should use it! Allen "Al" Davis was an American football coach and executive. He was the principal owner and general manager of the Oakland Raiders of the National Football League from 1972 to 2011. Under Davis' management, the Raiders became one of the most successful teams in professional sports. His motto for the team was "Just win, baby." Davis was active in civil rights, refusing to allow the Raiders to play in any city where black and white players had to stay in separate hotels. He was the first NFL owner to hire an African American head coach and a female chief executive. He was also the second NFL owner to hire a Latino head coach. He remains the only executive in NFL history to be an assistant coach, head coach, general manager, commissioner and owner. I respect people like him R.I.P Al Davis but individuals like that inspire young men like me to become motivational and evolutionary! So, I created Prince Motivation to let you completely in my world and shared with you my life struggles pain and fun moments. The biggest pain that I face daily is knowing that I didn't have the proper guidance in life. I found it thru politicians, music artists, and former athletes. Having to deal with being an outside child that was created out of wed lock makes you look at your life and say why was I kept a secret? Why did my mother have to raise me by herself? It motivates me to be great, and it lead to me writing this book. I visited my grandfather grave in 2015 and 2016. I haven't been there since I was nine years old. It took me that long to go see my real father who was there for me. I knew after our conversation at the grave yard that with all the current events going on, that I can use my story to reach someone who can relate to my story. I look at my life and say I made it to see thirty years of age. Was I ready to be a father back then when I didn't show the most upmost respect for a woman who said she was carrying my child? Or was I a boy running away from my responsibility that will eventually have my child write a book about me too? I want to publicly speak about stopping men from having children with women they have no love for. Creating life without love should be a crime. When you have real love, you have life!

This week I was on vacation and I arrange a dinner with my two brothers who reside in Dallas, Texas. We had great time sharing how we met our father. We reached out on our own and met up to discuss how we found out about our father who we shared. I love my father and I'm glad he gave me life. I do not like the fact that I only got to know after the fact I went thru pain and not having is knowledge or guidance. All three of sat at the table and for a moment I said, we all turned out alright. My younger brother Bryon Desinor is a God fearing, great ACTIVE father of three kids and married. My six-month older brother Junior Desinor is a very successful realtor business owner in the state of Texas. He is married to a beautiful wife and have two beautiful children. He also is a great active father. My older sister Kettia Desinor is a beautiful lady inside and out. She is the person who is responsible for introducing me to Bryson and group all of us together. Her soul is so beautiful she is another person who gives me advise and help me see the joy and pride in our situation. I have a brother also in Haiti name Stephane Desinor but we barely speak because I haven't mastered my Creole yet. So, I have a big family it's just spread out all over. I just must find my queen and make sure we keep all our love in our house. The importance of guidance and leading people you care about should never be short change.

I found Prince Motivation thru all my trials and tribulations. Would I have the work ethic that I have if I did have to pay my own bills. Would I be so positive if I did not sit in them jail cells? It's like as I wrote this book it was destine for me to graduate from everything I been thru. It bothers me when people say, "Dawg I'm a real Nigga till I Die" "Free All the Real Niggas" "he aint no Real Nigga" Let me make myself loud and clear. The last Real nigga I saw was on documentary when the KKK were hanging my ancestors from trees. You know the niggas that had shackles on they feet. The ones who obeyed they master so they can be alive for one day. The ones Willie Lynch Letter wrote in 1712 in Virginia about controlling slaves for years in modern day slavery. Those are the real niggas. These people that pride themselves off that title are simply miss guided. I got disappointed when I saw Young Thug on an album cover "Jeffery "with a dress. They call it fashion I call it humiliating a strong black man that has a platform to inspire the future. That to me hurt and motivated me to grow my platform. Being a young black male in 2000s is the scariest task to do these days, and we had a black president at the time. I think we have been had. Obama did a great job, he is a great father, and he proposed a lot of things that didn't get past. Us African Americans want Freedom, Justice, and Equality and I think we didn't receive those key things under his term. I'll leave it at that.

It was times in my life where I struggled. When I was a kid in middle school. I had food on the table but I didn't have the nicest shoes and clothes. My mom did the best she could. When I graduated high school, I can never forget riding my bike with my blue Urban League of Broward County book bag with no place to call home. I struggled with depression I felt that no one loved me. I felt things that I put on myself because I was alone. People like Lander Coleman, Vita Roland, Dwayne Roland, Delroy Lindsey Sr., Carmen Lindsey, Marcus Cadette, Melinda Cadette, Kenny Royster, Moultrie Green, were people who let me live with them when I had no place to call home. Until I could keep and afford a house on my own.

I said earlier that I was motivated my politics and music to create Prince Motivation. I want to speak on music right now. Sometimes I'm amazed by how an old song can play on the radio or from my CD player, and I can recite word for word. When I was in school, I was a bad test taker, and couldn't even remember what I needed to know for a quiz or test. That's how I know music sparks and has my ears and attention. I believe that we all in the black community, sometimes fall victim to the music we create and listen to. In some cases, I listen to trap music and gangster rap and don't get me wrong it sounds good. One day I was on the internet, YouTube to be exact and I put my laptop on mute and watch a rap video. It was an upcoming rapper, with his crew or as Phil Jackson will call it "Posse." (A body of men, typically armed, summoned by a sheriff to enforce the law). I think when he called Lebron James crew that it may have insulted him. It was a low budget video, shot in a poverty environment, the young men had they shirts off, had guns, they gang affiliated bandanas, mean mugging, and waving and pointing their guns to the camera. I learned that precipitation plays a huge part of how you portray yourself, and how others look at you. In this case, I guess they wanted to scare or impress the opposition or fans. To show how hard or how tough they are.

So, then I un muted the video and watch it all over again. This time I would listen to the hear what the rapper was saying in his lyrics, that he was spitting. You can tell he was a rookie, and his rhymes was typical and elementary to me. The lyrics was pretty much Fuck a Nigga, kill a Nigga, Pussy ass Nigga, I'll do this to a Nigga, if a Nigga try me, etc. Kevin Gates said once in an interview that exhibited of violence isn't always the best to deal with a situation. You don't always have to be so quick to fight or argue just because you dis-agree with somebody. Be a man of understanding and learn how to walk away, so you can live another day. So, after I watch the video two times once with music, and once just visually it hit me. My generation, culture, and these big record companies are literally encouraging killing and humiliating our own kind.

Sometimes we all fall victims to living, and speaking the same way the slave masters, ancestors, and supporters did during the four hundred years of slavery. When artist like the late great Tupac Shakur started to understand the power of the words, and the effect they have on a huge population. They started to clean up the message, yeah, they will make a radio hit because back then that was a way to put out music. Music has evolved and know you can drop music from your cell phones these days, and you don't have to be as talented. When they started to do interviews, and start to encourage our race, those records got no plays or spins. We let social media or media in public ridicule him (Tupac) judge him, and ultimately some brother somewhere killed our brother Tupac.

Same song as my brother Malcom X he was becoming a political leader. He started to realize in his religion that his religion loved everyone no matter the color of their skin. He started to realize that he must be smarter with his words when he spoke to the public and media outlets at the time. Our own raced kill Malcom X another strong educated leader that wanted to empower his people. When I put a post on social media that's probably negative or just entertaining it may get a whole bunch of likes, but when I put a paragraph of uplifting or motivating my people it gets no likes. I wonder if I become great at public speaking, or a successful author will I get killed by my own kind too?

A reason why I started Prince Motivation is to bring awareness from what I saw and witness growing up. I love Black People and care for all my brothers and sister, because I know the injustice and in sensitive times we go thru while on this thing we call earth. If I can't reach one individual God forbid something happen to me. That they get to this point in the book the very end and understand. I see where Prince Paul messed up, and I'm not going to make the same mistakes he made. I'm going to take his advice, and do better. I won't let other people influence me to always follow the crowd. I will use my platform responsibly. I will treat my companion with love and care. Treat he or she like a king or queen. I will try to be more positive in life, and try to find good in things. Young Jeezy said in a song long time call F.A.M.E "Can't slow down, too much evil in my rear view, sometimes you want to scream to God, but he can't hear you, and even if you did, this'll probably be his answer, "Fuck you 'complaining about? It aint like you got cancer".

When some at the workplace gets that promotion that they didn't deserve. You will have the power to not quit. Why on earth do people on earth stop making money because somebody else got something you didn't? You don't have goals, or kids to feed, or bills to pay? I rather you quit after you find a better opportunity or find something more beneficial. Sometimes the grass isn't always greener on the other side. Sometimes money shouldn't always determine where you should work. I want you all to know quality of life, and having a piece of mind is way more valuable than making an extra dollar or two! Whenever I have kids with a beautiful queen, I want my kids to know that I won't beat the shit out of them. That's the same thing the slave masters did to the slaves when they didn't do what they what they want. I'm not a parent and I do not raise your children, so with all respect and love I'm not telling you how to discipline your kids, but I will challenge parents to try something else if whooping and beating your children doesn't get the same result.

Its deep people the paranoia I have comes from all the events that happen in my life. A lot of people have the mindset of let me hurry up and have kids because I don't want to be to old! Really? I'm no one to judge, but how about before I fully mature, or when I meet the person God has picked or brought into my life. Until I am in a finically place in my life where I'm not living off government assistance, and can't make over a certain amount of money. I had my scare already, and that to me was a way for God to tell me, be careful Paul. Slow down for you wreck out, you and Bruce keep pulling out! I wasn't ready to be a father; you haven't met your queen yet. God told me Paul when I send her your way, she won't be perfect nobody is. Learn how to face an obstacle, learn how to take criticism from someone who cares and loves you.

I wasn't ready for most of my promotions because I acted emotionally and passionate at the wrong times. In business, you must take your personal feelings out of decision making. In some cases, I reacted to situations instead of shutting up and listening to a person teaching me something that I didn't know. I made people in higher positions feel like there is no helping me. That alone made me take longer to get to where I wanted to be in the company I work for. Everything I went thru was self-inflecting. I share all this with you, all because I see it daily. No matter what skin color you are or race or whatever religion you believe in. I notice when people debate or have difference in opinion. People don't stop and say, "You know what, why does that person feel like this? When do you realize that your life was not like theirs? If you never been racially profiled, you couldn't have the same opinion of someone who has. Where does respect come into play? Nobody is right or wrong when they are sharing opinions and beliefs, only facts can justify debates!

I thank God, every day for him giving Bishop T.D Jakes the spiritual guidance for his message in "Let It Go"! Ever since I saw his video on YouTube Let It Go by Bishop TD Jakes that was about 45 minutes long. It changed my life. You cannot hold grudges, it will stop your growth, your advancement, your real blessing. I would never have kids if I keep replaying what happen to me in 2007-2008. I must let it Go! When January 2016 came a brand-new year, it started off very rough for me. My roommate at the time passed away. My mother was in the hospital for her lungs because of smoking, fighting for her life. Her vision was deteriorating, and now my mother has glaucoma. The woman I was in the relationship with at the time that wanted to leave me. I had no choice but to let her go. I had a choice to make, is this person worth fighting for? Did I do her or her family wrong? Does this person represent myself and my brand well long term? I saw a few things that told me No. She wasn't for me, and that's cool. I still wish her well and may peace be upon her. I will continue to let go of people, places, and things that do not have a positive effect of change in my life. I will fight for love and people who are worth keeping or fighting for!

Prince Motivation is a way of life. I started off with nothing and ended up with everything I wanted in life materialistic wise. I use my smile and energy around others to show that a kid with no guidance can be a success story and not a statistic. I could've use the excuse I aint have my daddy in my life like some people, but I chose to say then what? When you faced with adversity the last thing you should say is, "Now what do or will I do?" One day, I sat and ate lunch with an elite group of individuals'. I worked and grinded with this group for years in my career. I remember listening to Bishop T.D Jake's saying he use to sit in meetings and see executive's n CEO's argue and debate then go have lunch together and leave everything at the table. Learning how to separate business and personal feelings. I sat quiet with all these thoughts in my head. Then I ate some more quietly because I looked at the table and I was the only African American at that table of 13. That's less than 10%. Some may think it's not that big of a deal. It's a testimony of a vision I saw that was challenging coming up in retail. I have a responsibility to not let down anyone that help me in my career and believed in me. It was times and opportunities for me to leave and go work in an easier atmosphere but I have bigger goals and I don't quit at anything I do. I have not been as privilege as some and it's cool. I respect people that respect me. I know the way my life and society has been set up that I should work harder than individuals to get to where I must go. Just thought I'll share this with anyone that hates going to work. Sometimes people make you uncomfortable at work so you can't be on their level or make what they make. I'm here to tell you anyone can make it in any field or career path!

My grandmother from another mother told me yesterday before I left the house. I kiss her on the cheek and said, "how you are feeling grandma"? as I left to go to work. She looked at me and said, "Some days you feel good some days you fight" I don't know if you caught that. I did she didn't say some days are good and some are bad. Some days you fight! Fight so the day don't feel bad. Fight for what or who you love. Her positive outlook makes her fight so her mind doesn't look at anything bad. You don't give up on your dreams or friend ships or relationships or sports or your health. You fight for everything! I'm not in the Hall of fame of anything but I know I'm on to something. Whether it's with the field I'm in now or the avenue I'm pursuing. You can be motivated by your children, or even an older person who can't get up and work no more. You can learn from anybody; you just should be open and listen! My family never was rich, never had reunions. My thoughts this morning was live a long healthy life and carrying my last name for many years to come the right way. I'm not ashamed of anything I've done, posted on social media, or people I let in and out of my life. It's call life you learn from every experience. I pretty much don't care about people opinions that don't matter. I'm proud of my nationality and my position in life right now. I sacrificed a lot of time and money in many different things, people, and places. Now it's time to invest all my time and energy in myself. So, what if someone doesn't like it. I will live long and will be great I have a goal to show everyone that think bad, to show them how great I am. You don't need approval for living your life after you become an adult. You

must make adult decisions and educate yourself on the consequences behind every permanent or temporary decisions you make. I don't live for yesterday, I live for today, tomorrow, and if I'm blessed to see another day! A man stands for something, supports his last name, walks with confidence, and earns respects!

Best thing I ever did was fall out of love, with someone who didn't keep it 100! Think about how can someone who really loves you, goes from loving everything about you to hating you, and all you ever did was love that person? Your heart doesn't lie, people do! When you love someone one it's a choice. You choose to love someone, you choose to accept their flaws, you choose to stay, you choose to fight to make it last forever. Love never leaves, the person just chooses to go love someone else. I want to talk about that word Love. What is your definition of Love? I love you is the worst lie you can tell somebody! Heart break is an emotion just like love is an emotion, we all go through these emotions. The hard thing is finding that real and true unconditional love! Watching people get engage is refreshing! Love is beautiful n sometimes it hurts! People who find it and keep it are very strong and understanding! Love is the support I got from friends and family that bought a Prince Motivation shirt before this book came out. Love is the support I got from people who every gave me positive truthful advice that I needed to here in life. Love is what I have for all people. I love who love me, and I love people that appreciate the word Love. The things we desire, desire us- Kevin Gates! You can want a new car, new house, marriage, new career, but you really should want it for yourself! Be cautious where you invest your money, time, heart, body, and effort. One thing about life is. It's easy to go through something and quit, give up, throw in the towel. One thing about pain is it doesn't last forever. Take a little pain, go thru something, go thru some adversity. Sometimes fighting for something, or going thru something makes you stronger.

It's very important to have a foundation and support system to help you achieve whatever you want to do in life! A successful man is one who can lay a firm foundation with the bricks others have thrown at him—David Brinkley. I created Prince Motivation to encourage people, not be glorified because I'm human and its only one God I fear and believe in. I believe in God but not your God! All religions believe in a God they might just call him something different and that's cool. I respect and believe that anything that you believe in that makes you a better person, parent, athlete, teacher, leader, scholar, lawyer, nurse, doctor, citizen, employee, on earth is good or great for you. Prayer, Patience, and Persistence is in my daily message behind Prince Motivation. With these three things, we can use it to get and overcome anything. Prayer can be a form of religious practice, may be either individual or communal and take place in public or in private. It may involve the use of words, song or complete silence. When language is used, prayer may take the form of a hymn, incantation, formal creedal statement, or a spontaneous utterance in the praying person. There are different forms of prayer such as petitionary prayer, prayers of supplication, thanksgiving, and praise. Prayer may be directed towards a deity, spirit, deceased person, or lofty idea, for worshipping, requesting guidance, requesting assistance, confessing transgressions (sins) or to express one's thoughts and emotions. Thus, people pray for many reasons such as personal benefit, asking for divine grace, spiritual connection, or for the sake of others. Like I said early whoever you pray to. Just Do it like Nike just have a conversation with him. Believe in him or her and let them guide you when it comes to decision making, or with someone you trust. Keep your God that you pray to first in whatever you do, because you wouldn't be here, or even have the time or ability to read this book.

Patience the capacity to accept or tolerate delay, trouble, or suffering without getting angry or upset. They say Patience is a virtue, but all good things come to those who wait. A lot of things I have seen and witness, when people rush into things or get done. Usually end up very bad. I see a lot of people rushing into marriages, and are no longer married. I see women rushing into having kids, and now they are struggling single parents. I see managers get promoted, and wasn't properly train, now he or she is head over heels and are failing. It's like when you eat too fast and your stomach hurts, because you didn't have the time to properly digest it. In my lifetime, I notice that when you rush things, it doesn't always end well. Me and my brother James once or twice a week go running and walking at Vista View Park. When we first start going out there James used to out run me in laps, up n down hills. Me and James are very competitive, so I didn't like to lose. At that time, he invited me out there I wasn't in shape, I wasn't eating healthy, or exercising at the time neither. I was not in the best shape or taking care of my body. It wasn't till a whole year later where the roles switch. I start using my gym member ship more at LA Fitness, and start going more often for better health and to stay in shape. I started to go running on my days off, because a brother name Eric Thomas who I went to see at a seminar changed my mindset. Team No Days off. When I saw Eric Thomas on YouTube a video and speech. You must want to succeed as bad as you want to breathe! I learn from that video that most successful people don't watch television. The only thing I watch is sports because I played sports when I was younger and I enjoy being a part of a team. I enjoy winning and competing. I watch football and basketball preferably Dallas Cowboys and Los Angeles Lakers games. I saw the movie Jerry McGuire and I thought that would be the perfect job for me. I'm a hustler and I love sports. I don't watch the news as much, because to me I take it to personal, and I don't like the stupidity and ignorance of people. I do pay attention to current events.

One more thing on Patience is the fact that we have a new president, and it created an uproar. Before you take a deep breath, and start thinking C'mon Paul don't tell me you about to defend Donald Trump. Donald John Trump is an American businessman, television producer, and the

President-elect of the United States, scheduled to take office as the 45th president under the 20th amendment on January 20, 2017; he holds the distinction as the oldest man ever elected to the presidency, surpassing Ronald Reagan. Hear me out. Yes, I voted for Hillary Clinton! Hillary Diane Rodham Clinton is an American politician who was the First Lady of the United States from 1993 to 2001, the 67th United States Secretary of State from 2009 to 2013, and was the Democratic Party's nominee for President of the United States in the 2016 election. Yes, I voted for Hillary Clinton but Donald Trump won. A lot of registered voters use their vote that my ancestors died and walked miles, thrown in jail, and got beat up, hosed by police for it to go to some may call a waste of time. I say this because it hurt me when I saw pictures on Twitter and Instagram when people choose other and wrote in their personal name or Hennessey. Now I'm no dictator, but your vote is your civil right. I will never encourage people to do what I would do. If you ask me I will tell you what I would do. But I will never push my beliefs or what I feel is right to do. So, Donald Trump won. He ran a race, worked hard, and won. To me if anyone works hard, competes, does well and wins fairly, all I can do is Respect It. I'll give him a chance, and wish him and his family well. Some people need or deserve a chance and we live in a nation that gives citizens a land of opportunity.

Most of the times I tell people, the opinion of others does not explain who you are. How you conduct yourself, and the things you do describe your character. Donald Trump wasn't a politician when he starts running for office. He became frustrated like every other American in this country that grew tired of being let down, investing your vote and money into candidates who told the same lies and broken promises. When he steps into a different avenue he was judge as a politician. To me the reason he won is because of him wanting to help the economy and his work ethic. He sold his message, dream, and vision to people who wanted change. That group of people whom believed in him, and made sure that he got elected. See if you want change and you want to make an impact in a community or in this case a nation. You need unity! You must come together, and leave your personal feelings and do things as a team to get a bigger result. Millions of Americans voted! They didn't announce Donald Trump a winner off your vote or mines. Millions got together and said that's who we want! They said we going to use our resources, money, and power to help this man win.

Which brings me to my last Word Persistence! Persistence is a firm or obstinate continuance in a course of action despite difficulty or opposition. If you want anything in life you need to be persistent. I tell my employees that work for me. Nothing was handed to me, so I expect you all to go get whatever you want in life. If you see someone you are attracted to put in the work. You going to introduce yourself, you going to compliment them, you going to communicate with them. I never seen someone marry someone they never met besides the television show married at first sight. Being persistent is like giving effort and not quitting. A lot of times I didn't want to stay home on the weekend to work on this book. I took days off because a lot has happened and I need all the current events up until this date to make sure I finish what I started. In life, it's easy to quit. It's easy to take a play off. It's easy to call off work and not let people down. It's easy to break up with someone when they don't see things the same way you do. It's easy to run away from situations or your responsibility, but it takes some certain individuals to deal with adversity and situations. It's easy for me to follow the crowd and go be another ass kisser at work. It's easy to give up on life and live off the government. It's easy to go sell drugs and break into hard working people houses. I choose to leave you this book, leave you my story, leave you my legacy. This book was an idea, and I didn't want to die with it. I wanted to share it. I started saying yes to my dreams, and my potential. I want to accomplish my goals, and want to succeed. When adversity struck me, I gave up. I went into depression. I let people beat me. Now I understand that it's all about how much you can take, and get up. Quitting will last forever. When I started this book, I made sure quitting wasn't an option. I quit school in 2004, and I re-enroll in 2016. I'm going to complete everything I start. I will sacrifice what I want to become. At this point in my life I prefer peace than war, and love over hate. Prince Motivation will be my light away from my darkness. The light and individual that they look at, and say "if he can do it, so can I"! I hope my life, my story, my journey can help you. I give all praise to the highest for giving me the strength to write this book on my own, and publish this book on my own, finally I want to thank you for supporting Prince Motivation and taking the time out your life or schedule to read this. God, bless You all friend or Foe may peace be upon you! PRINCE

Author's note: All historical information and quoted material courtesy of Google.

71253254R00055

Made in the USA
Columbia, SC
27 May 2017